To
Sinead & Alex
with my best wishes
Chijii Chili
15/2/2011

AFRICAN CHRISTIANITY IN BRITAIN

Diaspora, Doctrines and Dialogue

Chigor Chike

Bloomington, IN 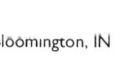  Milton Keynes, UK
authorHOUSE®

AuthorHouse™
1663 Liberty Drive, Suite 200
Bloomington, IN 47403
www.authorhouse.com
Phone: 1-800-839-8640

AuthorHouse™ UK Ltd.
500 Avebury Boulevard
Central Milton Keynes, MK9 2BE
www.authorhouse.co.uk
Phone: 08001974150

© 2007 Chigor Chike. All rights reserved.

No part of this book may be reproduced, stored in a retrieval system, or transmitted by any means without the written permission of the author.

First published by AuthorHouse 3/29/2007

ISBN: 978-1-4259-9686-4 (sc)

Printed in the United States of America
Bloomington, Indiana

This book is printed on acid-free paper.

Cover: A Zimbabwean Christian

To Obi

Table of Contents

	Foreword ix
	Preface xiii
Chapter 1	Introduction 1
Chapter 2	The use of the Bible 11
Chapter 3	The Doctrine of God 31
Chapter 4	The Doctrine of the Person of Christ 53
Chapter 5	The Doctrine of Salvation 75
Chapter 6	Theological Issues Raised 97
Chapter 7	Summary 111
Chatper 8	Concluding Observations 123
	Bibliography 127
	Appendix 149
	List of questions used during the interviews 150
	Index 153

FOREWORD

I owe a life long debt of gratitude for all I learned about Christian faith from eight years of life and ministry in Africa – a year in Kenya and seven years in Northern Nigeria as a Church Mission Society partner.

Chigor Chike, an ordained Nigerian minister now working in Newham, East London, writes about the experiences of African Christians living as minority communities in a predominantly white country. I have a particular sensitivity to their experience as Carole and I and two white colleagues were a minority of four in the Nupe Church which is now the Diocese of Bida. So much of what Chigor explores rings bells with that rich and challenging chapter of my ministry. His investigation draws from literature on the subject, the themes of contemporary African preachers and interviews with twenty African Christians chosen to reflect a wide diversity of denomination and nationality.

He speaks of the influence of a pre-Christian worldview upon the interpretation of Christianity by African Christians. This world-view is holistic and experiences the spiritual and material as one and the same rather than the often competing entities with which we westerners often struggle.

Africans instinctively experience God as a powerful, supernatural being who engages with the whole person and not just their souls as the missionaries tended to teach. Theirs is a God who is Creator, Provider, Healer and Judge. It is for this reason that many left the mission churches of CMS and USPG and set up independent churches that embraced this holistic emphasis which resonated with their traditional culture.

Jesus is encountered as, not so much the one who forgives sins, as a conqueror over evil spirits, witch-craft, magic, the devil and poverty.

Chigor rehearses the powerful place of Bible teaching and preaching in African Christianity. He speaks of the ease at which Africans weave their personal stories into the biblical narratives so that the Bible embraces the totality of their existence. There must be something of the craft of the praise singer here. This is perhaps a reason why a predominantly liberal and western interpretation of the Bible is causing offence for many African Christians over the issue of sexual morality.

Salvation in African Christianity is experienced in the broad, all encompassing way that I learnt about in my Old Testament studies but have failed to experience sufficiently in my day to day life-style. Is this because I have been blinkered by my western upbringing? My African friends have had a mere handful of decades of Christian inheritance to inform them. I have had two handfuls of centuries of inheritance to form me. Of the two sets of experience my view is that African Christians live closer to the world-view of the Bible than I who have been Christianised for so long but also liberalised and rationalised for so long.

One of the striking features which comes through Chigor's interviews is the gradual change that has taken place in African Christians during a period of twenty or more years of exposure to British Christianity. Those who Chigor interviewed who had left Africa for the United Kingdom within the past five years spoke of the Bible in stronger and more personal terms than those who have lived in Britain for more than twenty years. The liberalising tendency of British Society and Christianity has affected the way African Christians encounter God, Jesus, the Bible and salvation. Some of this change is for the better. Much, I fear, is for the worse.

Chigor summarizes the strengths of African Christianity as being a faith that is genuinely Incarnational and therefore able to engage with whatever social context believers move to. And it is a faith that has an integrated view of life.

The weakness he sees as a propensity, among some, to interpret salvation as being synonymous with material wealth – hence the term 'prosperity gospel'. In spite of the influential East African Revival of the 1930's and 40's a theology of the cross is now somewhat lacking. If the suffering and humiliation of Jesus were more prominent in their theology this might provide a healthy counterpoint to the prevalent emphasis on God's glory, Christ's victory, and the believers' prosperity.

There is much in this book to inform, provoke and challenge Christians of whatever ethnicity. We all struggle to find an authentic expression of Christianity through the filters of our national cultures. Some filters are more helpful than others. May this study stimulate us to help one another discover more of the Lord whom we worship and serve.

> David Hawkins
> Bishop of Barking
> February 2007

PREFACE

How Africans practise Christianity is a subject that has interested me for years. As I live in Britain, another dimension of that interest has been whether the Christian beliefs and practices of Africans were being affected by their experience of living in Britain. In 2000, I started collecting and studying books written by African preachers in both Africa and Britain. A three-year Master of Theology programme at Oxford gave me the perfect opportunity to carry out proper research into the subject. As part of that research, I interviewed twenty African Christians living in Britain. I chose the interviewees carefully to reflect the diversity of nationalities and denominations and the different lengths of time people have lived in Britain.

This research was something of a journey for me. Indeed, aspects of it have been a literal journey as I travelled to meet people for interviews. I suspect that the quest has been partly motivated by questions from deep inside me — perhaps questions to do with a changing identity, pulled on one side by my roots in Africa and on the other by my life in Britain. The study focuses on how this tug-of-war plays out in the Christian faith of Africans (including myself) and shows that although the African heritage within Christianity is very robust, over a long period of time, the British context has a noticeable effect on the faith of Africans. My hope is that this book will be useful to people who have interest in the variety of expressions of Christianity around the world.

I would like to thank Walter Houston, who supervised the dissertation at Oxford on which this book is based, David Whitehead for reading through and offering advice, my wife, Obi, and the children for their support and Almighty God for making it all possible.

CC
London, 2007.

Chapter 1

Introduction

What is African Christianity?

Contrary to what many people today might think (Africans included), Africa has had a long involvement with Christianity. It is noteworthy that the list of nations mentioned in the Biblical account of the coming of the Holy Spirit in the book of Acts includes Egypt and Libya[1]; the Evangelist Mark is traditionally believed to have established the church in Egypt in AD 42[2]; in the first seven centuries of the Christian era, the northern third of Africa, as well as Ethiopia and much of Sudan was predominantly Christian,[3] and this early involvement gave the Christian religion African saints such as Clement, Augustine, Origen, Athanasius and Tertullian.[4] However, the spread of Christianity to sub-Saharan Africa (which is where it is now thriving in Africa, much of the north having converted to Islam) has mainly been the work of Western missionaries. The big expansion took place in the nineteenth century, which is sometimes called "the Age of

Mission"[5]. One imagines that many Africans are grateful to these missionaries for that, but it has also become clear that the missionaries got some things wrong.

Many European and American missionaries to sub-Saharan Africa adopted a "blanket" condemnation of all aspects of African culture rather than trying to understand the African way of thinking. For example, in Tanzania, many missionaries

> proscribed important elements of African culture and practices, describing them as anti-religious…So that becoming Christian always meant, in part, setting oneself off from the inheritance of the past.[6]

Similarly, among the Chaga of the Kilimanjaro (also in Tanzania), missionaries branded many aspects of the community's life as "primitive", "pagan", "heathen" or "savage" and sought to eradicate them.[7] They tried to replace the Chaga's "awareness of the universalism of all life" with a European outlook that divided life into physical and spiritual compartments.[8] Some of this has been attributed to a simple inability of the European missionaries to separate the essence of the Christian gospel from the European culture that had penetrated it for more than a thousand years.[9] But some scholars, like Gregory Maddox, have seen a political motivation: Maddox points out that "Mission in Africa was politically the `handmaiden' of colonialism and often reinforced obedience to the new colonial order".[10] In other words, the suppression of African culture by European missionaries aided the political domination of Africa by Europeans.

Increasing political, cultural and theological awareness has led many Africans to leave the churches set up by missionaries, such as the Roman Catholic, Anglican and Methodist churches (sometimes called "mission" or "historical" churches), to form their own churches. These new African churches try to weave into their Christian beliefs and practices the characteristics of traditional African ways of life, such as:

1 a sense of community, for example, finding identity and meaning in life through extended family ties;
2 important relationships with the spirits of their ancestors;
3 a belief in a Supreme being;
4 a strong relationship between the spirit world and the physical world, and;
5 the view that human life is holistic, not divided into separate, unrelated elements.[11]

This has given rise to "African Christianity". For the churches and theologians fashioning it, broadly speaking, the goal is "to achieve integration between the African pre-Christian religious experience and African Christian commitment in ways that would ensure the integrity of African Christian identity and selfhood."[12] Early cases of these African Independent Churches (AICs)[13] include the Arathi, or Spirit, Churches of East Africa and the Aladura Church of West Africa, which emerged in the 1920s[14] and 1930s[15], respectively. Today, tens of thousands of AICs are in Africa, set up by Africans searching for a form of Christianity that rings true within them. Significantly, many of the "mission churches", even though they continue to maintain strong ties with

Europe, have started to allow the influence of African culture and tradition into their church life.

The Diaspora Effect

As part of the phenomenal movement of people around the world in recent decades, Africans have come to live in Britain in significant numbers. There is now the concept of an African Diaspora in Britain. The term "Diaspora" (galuth or golah, Hebrew meaning "exile") was originally used to refer to the dispersion of Jews beyond Israel, which had its beginnings in the Assyrian and Babylonian deportations of about 721 and 597 BC.[16] "Diaspora Jews" therefore refers to the Jews dispersed and consequently living among Gentiles. However, recent usage focuses on the idea of a community living as a minority in a foreign land. In Germany, for example, "Diaspora" refers to members of any religious body living as a minority among those of other beliefs.[17] In Black Studies, Roswith Gerloff has written about the "African diaspora from both sides of the Atlantic",[18] meaning black people living as minorities in Europe, who have come from either Africa or the Caribbean. It is in this sense of living as a minority in a foreign land that I am using the world "Diaspora." Within the black community in Britain, people often make a distinction between an "African" and an "African Caribbean"[19] — the former refers to those who have come to Britain from Africa, and the latter refers to those of African ethnic origin who have ancestry in the Caribbean. This is the way the term "African" is being used in this book.

The central argument of this book is that pressures within the British social context shape the Christianity practiced by Africans in Africa when it is brought to Britain. Many aspects of this discussion raise questions. For example, it is important to point out that even though I refer to "Africa", North Africa is largely Muslim. Also, South Africa, because of the experience of apartheid, has been on a different theological trajectory than the rest of sub-Saharan Africa. In a sense, black South Africans have experienced in their own country the social pressures that other Africans experience only in the Diaspora. I am also mindful of the differences between different African communities and the dangers of speaking about them as though the whole continent were one homogenous entity. But I agree with Mbiti and others[20] that there are sufficient similarities among African communities to justify some general treatment.

There is nowadays little doubt that context affects both Christian belief and Christian practice. Obvious examples in the West are be the way the First World War undermined the optimistic tendency in Liberal Theology in Europe and the greater acceptability of the idea that God suffers resulting from the reflections of Moltmann[21] and others on the suffering of the Second World War. The unsettling experience of moving from one continent to another, the experience of living in a culture different from that of one's formation, and the experience of racial discrimination[22] can in a similar way raise fundamental questions that demand a new theological response from Christians. In the words of Roswith Gerloff, who has studied African Christianity in Britain for many years, Africans tackle racial, cultural and religious conflicts in Europe daily with

> valour and tenacity of faith, not least derived from spiritual and cultural sources which, even

in displacement, allow for resistance, survival and freedom of expression.[23]

In the following chapters, I will discuss how this tenacious faith wrestles with issues that arise from the British context and what changes that context has produced.

The Focus on Doctrines

In carrying out this investigation, I will focus primarily on doctrines. Doctrine has to do with what a Christian believes about the self, others, the world and the supernatural.[24] It can be contrasted with the three other key aspects of the Christian religion: *Discipline*, which has to do with the structure of corporate life and the consequences of deviant behaviour; *Liturgy*, which has to do with worship, praise, music, prayer and the sacraments; and *Life*, which has to do with the individual life of the believer in prayer, study, devotion, work, etc.[25] These four areas are, obviously, related and affect one another. By focusing primarily on doctrines, I will concentrate on what African Christians believe rather than how they worship or live out their Christianity. However, because the areas are related, the study will also produce some insights into their practice.

Even though my focus is doctrine, I have included a chapter on the Bible. The book has been divided into the following chapters: a) the use of the Bible, because this promises to be an area of significant difference, b) doctrine of God, because theology, by definition, is about God, c) doctrine of Christ, because this is the centre of Christian theology, d) doctrine of Salvation, because this is another area where Africans are distinctive in their approach, and e) an evaluation of biblical and theological issues raised. I will begin each chapter by describing the situation in Africa, and complement the existing works of scholars of African Christianity with my own analysis of recent publications by African Christian preachers based in Africa. In the British scene, where very little study has been done in this area, I will be relating the results of (a) my study of books and sermons published by a cross section of British-based African preachers, (b) findings from twenty interviews I conducted of a cross section of African Christians and ministers in Britain (see Appendix), (c) a study of materials such as the racism resource packs of different churches and (d) unpublished dissertations at university libraries. In both Africa and Britain, I will be looking at material from a variety of countries and church denominations. My case for the effect of the Diaspora phenomenon will be based on i) a comparison between what I find in these two contexts (especially the work of Independent Church preachers in the two contexts) and ii) a comparison of the views of Africans who have lived in Britain for varying periods of time to see how those who have lived in Britain for a long period have been influenced by the British context

The Need for Dialogue

The existence of an identifiable "African Christianity" with the prospect of further colouration by the British context raises a number of questions. A key question is whether it is ever right for Christianity to get such a qualification as "African". One may ask whether

Christianity should not be one, just as God is one, and Jesus Christ is one. Furthermore, if qualifications are to be allowed, how does one decide what is in and what is out? In other words, to what extent can what is permissible within the Christian family be stretched? These questions are arising more and more with increased contact by people from different regions of the world. I will consider evidence suggesting that Christianity isn't the same around the world . And I will consider ideas for deciding how to agree on what can rightly be regarded as Christian and what cannot. In that context, I will consider the idea that dialogue has a key role to play in holding the Christian family together.

Chapter 1 Endnotes

[1] J Mbiti, *Bible and Theology in African Christianity* (Nairobi: Oxford University Press, 1986) p1.

[2] ibid.

[3] Ibid, p1.

[4] ibid.

[5] A Wessels, *Images of Jesus*: (Grand Rapids, Michigan: Eerdmans Publishing Co., 1990) p100.

[6] G Maddox "The Church and Cigogo: Fr Stephen Mlundi and the Church in Central Tanzania" in *East African Expressions of Christianity* ed. T Spear and I Kimambo (Oxford: James Currey Ltd, 1999), p152.

[7] A A Lema, "Chaga Religion and Missionary Christianity on Kilimanjaro: The Initial Phase, 1893–1916" in *East African Expressions of Christianity* ed. T Spear and I Kimambo (Oxford: James Currey Ltd, 1999), p52.

[8] Ibid.

[9] ibid.

[10] Maddox, *East African Expressions*: 153.

[11] O'Donovan: 4.

[12] Bediako, 2000: 49.

[13] Sometimes the word "Indigenous", "initiated" or "instituted" is used.

[14] Githieya: 231.

[15] Mbiti, 1986: 35.

[16] *Oxford Dictionary of the Christian Church*: 477.

[17] Ibid.

[18] R Gerloff, "Editorial": 275.

[19] See e.g. Sturge, 2005: 53.

[20] Mbiti, 1969: 1; Parratt, 1995: 59; O'Donovan: 4.
[21] See Moltmann, 1974.
[22] For more on British racism, see for example, Peter Fryer: 391–399.
[23] Gerloff, 2000: 5.
[24] "Spirituality" in NDT: 657.
[25] Ibid.

Chapter 2

The use of the Bible

2.1 Introduction

In this chapter, I will compare the importance of the Bible to Africans in Africa and Britain and how they use the book to see what effect the British context might be having on Africans in Britain. I will begin by establishing the situation in Africa, including looking at any evidence suggesting that African Christianity in Africa is distinctive in this respect. Then I will compare and contrast this with the situation in Britain and consider reasons for any differences I find.

2.2 The Bible in Africa

Much existing evidence shows that a determination to stay close to the Bible is a common feature of African Christianity. Indeed, as I observed when I was living in

Africa, many Africans literally stay close to their Bibles, carrying them as they go about their daily business. This is often indicative of something more profound, a commitment to practice a Christianity that is Biblical from first to last. African churches commonly undertake regular Bible study in addition to Sunday services, and many of the songs they sing in church are based on verses of the Bible. Since the 1960s, many studies have confirmed the central role the Bible has in the faith of African Christians. In the mid-1960s, David Barrett, after an "exhaustive" survey of AICs in Africa stated that the Bible, more than anything else, was at the centre of their life and development.[1] H W Turner, in his study of the Aladura, which included an analysis of 8,000 sermons, found not only extensive use of the Bible but also use of every single book of the Bible.[2] The Aladura constitution makes clear this commitment to Biblical Christianity. It states:

> the scriptures are the official basis of the church, and an effort is made to support practice and teaching by biblical references. The church desires to be a biblical church and holds the Bible in great reverence.[3]

During the 1970s, as more Africans got involved in the study of African Christianity, they not only observed but encouraged this commitment to the Bible. Edward Fashole Luke saw the Bible as "the basic and primary source for the development of African Christian theologies".[4] African theologians, collectively, in Accra, Ghana, in 1977, declared the Bible as "the basic source of African theology, because it is the primary witness of

African Christianity in Britain

God's revelation in Jesus Christ."[5] The following decade, in 1986, John Mbiti found in his own study that "African Christianity is Biblically grounded"[6] and the influence of the Bible was still spreading. He writes,

> the Bible is making indelible marks on the religious scene in Africa. It is read widely, it is expounded from pulpits, street corners, market places, on radio and television, as well as in a wide range of publications.[7]

My own study of recent publications by African preachers shows that this commitment to a Biblical Christianity continues today. Faced with congregations for whom the main, if not sole, authority of Christian truth is the Bible, the custom is for the preacher to support every point with a Biblical reference. For example, the Ghanaian preacher, Dr Charles Agyin-Asare, who is Presiding Bishop of a network of about 300 churches in Ghana, in his book, *Power in Prayer*[8], quotes the Bible about one hundred and thirty four times, to support more or less every point. David Oyedepo, the General Overseer of the Nigeria-based Living Faith Ministry,[9] whose 50,000 capacity worship centre fills up every week, in his book, *The Miracle Seed*,[10] quotes the Bible, coincidentally, one hundred and thirty four times. These examples illustrate the importance of scripture in African Christianity.

Apart from this tendency to frequently quote the Bible, another practice that can be considered evidence of their high regard for the Bible is the highlighting or indenting of Biblical texts to give them prominence. We find this, for example, in Dr. Agyin-Asare's books, *The*

Impact of Prayer[11] and *Power in Prayer,* and in the book, *The Release Procedure*[12] by another Ghanaian, Kingsley Vander-Puije, in the work of many Kenyan preachers, such as Paul Nyamu's *The Holy Spirit,*[13] James Kiranga's *The Ultimate Weapon in Spiritual Warfare*[14] and Alan Kiuna's *Created for Dominion.*[15] Another practice is to quote huge blocks of text from the Bible, as we find in *Divine Encounter*[16] by Pastor E Adeboye, the Overseer of the Redeemed Christian Church, described as the "fastest growing church in Nigeria".[17] He repeats the same pattern in *Showers of Blessings*.[18] Other examples are *A Woman of Noble Character* by the Kenyan Faith Nthiga and *The True Way to Overcome Satan's Opposition* by the Kenyan preacher Edward Mwai.

Reading the work of these African preachers can make one feel as if the Bible is not just being used to support a case but is itself the case. The Bible is held in such high regard that even when providing answers to practical social problems, they do not undertake a social analysis, but simply provide Biblical passages or stories as answers. For example, the Nigerian preacher, Adeboye, in addressing the issue of poverty in his society, commended his book *Divine Encounter* as a way out because it is "based firmly on Biblical principles and characters"[19] and went on to tell stories of Old Testament characters overcoming adversity to encourage people out of poverty. This love for OT stories is another important feature of how the Bible is used by African Christians in Africa.

African Christians in using Biblical texts have a tendency to weave their personal story with stories in the Bible:

> The sentence of death over Jacob's life was cancelled
>
> …may you have an encounter with God which will cancel every threat of death
>
> God changed Jacob's name to bring him good fortune
>
> …Today, God will change whatever name that is working against you.[20]

In the same way, African Christians, not just the preachers, weave their personal story with stories in the Bible. Because they do not see the Bible primarily as a history book, they have no difficulty making their story part of Biblical stories or telling Biblical stories as if they were occurring today. One possible reason is that Africans think of time not as a linear phenomenon[21] but in cyclic terms. In their use of the Bible, great feats of contextualization are not usually necessary to relate Biblical events to present life or *vice versa*.

The following reasons have been given for why the Bible has become so important to African Christians:

1) For many Africans, the Bible brought Christianity home to them when it was translated into their mother tongue. It became their chief direct contact with Christian thought,[22] and they came to know God simply as the "God of the Bible".[23] In many cases, it was the first major publication in these languages,[24] and the act of translation was often a landmark in the history of the church in the area.[25]

15

2) The traditional African worldview and the worldview of the Bible are quite similar. As in the Bible, Africans experience the physical and spiritual aspects of the world as constantly flowing into each other. So it is easy for Africans to attach the Biblical worldview to their traditional one and weave their individual stories into those of the Bible. They also feel affirmed in their cultural, social and religious life.

3) Reading the Bible for themselves put Africans on an equal footing with other Christians, including the white missionaries, and hence it empowered them to "continue in the fight for our full humanity".[26] It is not surprising that it was instrumental in the formation of the AIC movement.[27] The Arathi Church, which emerged in central Kenya in the mid 1920s,[28] was able to stand on the Bible to criticize the mission churches' encouragement of servitude[29] and to condemn the colonization of Kenya as something God was against.[30] In Mbiti's words, the Bible gives Africans "liberation from ready-made and imported Christianity, liberation to generate the kind of Christianity which more fully embraces the totality of their existence."[31]

2.3 The British Experience

A study of books written by British-based African Christians shows that the way Africans in Africa regard and use the Bible is retained to a large extent by those

African Christianity in Britain

in Britain — the frequent quotations, highlighting of Biblical texts, use of big blocks of Biblical texts, frequent use of Old Testament stories and interweaving personal and Biblical stories all occur much the same way among African Christians in Britain as they do among those in Africa. Matthew Ashimolowo's book *So You Call Yourself a Man*[32] and Edmund Anyahamiwe's book *Flesh of God*[33] are examples of the frequent use of quotations. Just like the African-based preachers, Albert Odulele of Glory House in London highlights Biblical texts in such books as *Living by Faith — Move your mountains*[34] and *Understanding God's Voice.*[35] Ebianga Frank-Briggs also uses highlighting in *Unbreakable Laws of Faith,*[36] as does D and S Aggrey-Solomon's *The Courtship that Leads to Marriage.*[37] Odulele uses the same big blocks of Biblical text found in the Africa-based preachers in his book *Eternity Unveiled.*[38] The same love for the Old Testament found in Africa-based preachers such as Adeboye and groups like the Aladura[39] and the Arathi[40] can be seen, for example, in Ashimolowo's use of the person of Boaz as a model of a good man, Lawrence Tetteh's[41] use of David's story to discuss the anointing of God[42] and Albert Odulele's use of the story of Joshua to teach about divine guidance.[43] Similarly, the tendency to weave the life of today with Biblical stories can be seen, for example, in this proclamation by Pastor Vincent Odulele (the brother of Albert Odulele) to the congregation of Glory House in Plaistow London:

> I will make you a great nation
> kings and queens will come out from your loins
> I will make you so great your greatness will be a

>blessing to nations
>People, groups, continents will be touched by your greatness
>God says I will bless those that bless you
>Just because people are your friends they will be great because of your greatness.[44]

Here he weaves God's blessing of Abraham (in Gen 17:6) with his own blessing of the congregation. This phenomenon can, in fact, be observed among other people of African descent. African slaves in America achieved the same goal by giving Biblical names to key locations or people involved in their story — for example, referring to the woods where they met secretly to pray as "wilderness", the northern parts of the USA and Canada where they could escape to freedom as "Canaan" and the Ohio River, which was their route to physical freedom, as the "River Jordan".[45] By so doing, they made their story one with that of the Bible. We can term this practice of making personal stories part of the story of the Bible, Biblification. By *biblifying* their personal story, Africans, past and present, are able to see their daily life experience as a spiritual battle, which is their natural way of operating.

In spite of these similarities between Africans in Africa and those in Britain, my study uncovered two changes that result from the change in context. The first relates to the use of human reason as a source of theology. Four main areas have been generally accepted as authoritative sources of Christian truth: Scripture, Reason, Tradition and Experience.[46] Although both the Africans in Africa and those in Britain give similar weight to Bible, Experience and Tradition (giving much to the first, some to the second and very little to the third), they differ in the amount of weight they give to Reason. My analysis of books written by these two groups of African Christians shows that in general, African Christians in Britain are more likely to use Reason to support a proposition (in addition to the Bible and their experience and not instead of them) than their counterparts in Africa. For example, in her book *Satan-Proof Your Children*, Grace Akanle, an ordained minister based in Britain, discusses the Christian way of bringing up children with little recourse to the Bible, but rather relying on the reasonableness of her case. In one section, she criticizes parents who simply say "I don't know where he got that from",[47] pointing out that the parents have the ultimate responsibility for raising their children and would be judged by God for how well they have done it:

> God has entrusted into our care these young spirit beings we call children. They belong to God, but He has given us the duty of watching over them in this life. We are their caretakers and we are answerable to God.[48]

In another section, she advises parents to give their children time to reflect on their mistakes because "the need to understand step by step where a mistake lies, how they have gone off the track is important."[49] In this and other cases, she did not support her statements with Biblical quotations. Another example is Moses Owolabi's *Which God*, where he argues from reason and common sense for religious tolerance.

> We should not preach to or demand religious tolerance from other fellows when we ourselves

> behave in an intolerant and intolerable way. Violence should not be part of religion; it is an indication of one's need of a Saviour, and the proof that your religion is not working.[50]

As with Akanle, the sense is that these positions are being supported by commonly held truths or practical wisdom. The writer does not support the case with Biblical references.

This observation of a change from what Africans would normally do was supported by the results from the twenty people I interviewed. Although all those interviewed — no matter their length of stay in Britain, denomination or country of origin — spoke of the Bible as God's manual for living comparable to nothing else in Christianity, those who left Africa within the past five years or less spoke of the Bible in stronger terms. Three people described the Bible as "life" or "my life." One of them said, "As a Christian, the Bible to me is life. It means that I cannot live without talking to God or God talking to me and it is through the Bible that I can do this". In contrast, those who have been here more than twenty years showed more awareness of some of the reservations that have been raised about the Bible, such as the charge that it is outdated and the need to consider the context of Biblical precepts. For example, on homosexuality, one person said that although they do not think it is right:

> The way that it might have been dealt with in the Old Testament is obviously different from the way we have to deal with it today. We have to be compassionate. We have to basically remember that at the end of the day that God is love.

When people were asked to compare African Christians in Africa with African Christians in Britain, many felt those in Africa were more likely to focus exclusively on the Bible and to interpret it literally. One person made this comparison based on her experience of ministering in both Africa and Britain:

> In Britain, people do not believe in taking the Bible word for word…most of what we do in Africa is Biblically based. But here there is a lot more of Reason and people want it to be explained in contemporary terms, which is good.

This suggests that Africans in Britain are being influenced by the epistemological traditions (i.e., acceptable ways of knowing) of their present context. In Britain and much of Europe, especially since the Enlightenment, people accept human logic as authoritative. Many people are sceptical of the supernatural. Africans appear to imbibe this tendency to judge and accept what is truth on the basis of what is logical.

The second change pertains to the use of the Bible to address the issue of racism. This practice may not be widespread yet, but it is happening. For example, the Malawian born theologian Patrick Kalilombe, who lived in Britain for a number of years, described the church's Gospel message as a key weapon in the fight against racism[51] and in an article about his life and faith in Britain drew constantly on the Bible to challenge racism. He began by pointing out that his determination to share his story and the hope he has as "a black Catholic" derives from 1 Pet 3: 15–16[52]. He quotes Eph 4:4–5 ("one Lord, one faith, one baptism") to support the case that all Christians are one because they belong to one Lord.[53] And he quotes John 11:52 to support the case that the diversity of people in Britain is not a bad thing but a foreshadow of God's kingdom.[54] In some cases, the Bible is used not so much for "fighting" racism but for consoling its victims. For example, writing about the discrimination that black people face in mental health treatment, Bernard Nwulu quoted Mk 2:17 ("It is not the healthy who need a doctor, but the sick") to point out the need to help black people whose self esteem has been undermined by prolonged ill-treatment.[55] Another African Christian, Obi Igwara, described herself, among other things, as a poor, black woman and stated that even if the world despises her, God will not because based on Gen 1:26–31, when God created her, "He saw that I was very, very good and he blessed me".[56]

The sign that this phenomenon is no longer confined to theology books is Pastor Ashimolowo's recent series, *Black and Blessed*.[57] Ashimolowo devoted the whole month of October in 2004 and 2005 to preaching against racism, and it is fair to say that his sword for the fight was the Bible. He presented substantial Biblical evidence to challenge those who interpret Gen 9:18–27 to mean that black people were cursed by Noah. As signs of achievement by black people, he referred to Gen 10:8 to Nimrod, the son of Cush, a great man who built many cities. He also quoted Jer 13:23, "can the Ethiopian change his skin", to argue that people are who God made them and Gen 1:31 ("and God saw that everything he created was good") to argue that black people stand with all of humanity as equally pleasant before God. Even if one accepted that black people were cursed by Noah, he argues, Gal 3:13 ("Christ has redeemed us from the curse of the law…and the blessing of Abraham rests upon us") and 2 Cor 5:17 ("if any man be in Christ he is a new creature, old things have passed away") imply that such a curse has been removed by Jesus Christ. Whatever are the merits or otherwise of Ashimolowo's case, what is obvious is that this is a substantial deployment of the Bible in the fight against racism.

In fact, examples of black people using the Bible to resist oppression go back to the fight against slavery and the slave trade in the eighteenth and nineteenth centuries. Olaudah Equiano, who came to Britain as a slave from what is now Nigeria, often used the Bible in his memoirs as the basis of his argument for abolition. For example, he recalled how brothers often wept bitterly as they were sold to separate masters, knowing they would never see each other again, and asked: "O, ye nominal Christians, must not an African ask you, learned you this from your God, who says unto you, do unto all men as you would men should do onto you?"[58] He thus challenged the white population with the Golden Rule (Matt 7:12). In another instance, after describing how white people steal from black men and rape black women, he warns the white people of God's judgment and in reference to Luk 4:18f asks: "if these are not the poor, the broken hearted, the blind the captive, the bruised which our Saviour speaks of, who are they?" Another ex-slave, Ottobah Cugoano, used the creation story of Genesis to argue that no part of humanity is inferior to another since "mankind did spring from one original",[59] the same point Ashimolowo and Kalilombe would make two hundred years later. Cugoano also used the Bible to argue for a rest day for slaves every seven days.[60]

2.4 Issues raised by the African use of the Bible

Two issues stand out in how Africans use the Bible. The first is their frequent quoting of it born out of a commitment to Biblical Christianity. The feeling appears to be that they cannot go wrong if they stay close to the Bible. But this could be mistaken because Biblical texts are always subject to different interpretations. Controversies in Christian history have not necessarily arisen because one of the groups involved was not using the Bible, but because the groups have different interpretations of the Bible. That is why tradition, reason and experience are used alongside the Bible in theological reflection. The African Christianity that has been discussed in this study is relatively new, so traditions have not bedded down. It is also understandable that African Christians may not want to gulp down all the traditional positions that have been formulated out of other people's questions. It is, however, important that they work to develop their own questions and traditions.

The second issue is the tendency to weave their story with those of the Bible without a rigorous process and with only a superficial attention to the original context of the story. This could be seen as disregarding the intended meaning of the text. For Africans, however, this practice is not arbitrary or born out of laziness, but part of the pattern observed above. They are able to weave Biblical stories with their own because, in many ways, the Biblical world is like theirs.[61] In both, the physical and the spiritual aspects of the world are seen as constantly flowing into each other. The practice is also possibly related to the traditional African concept of human life in relation to time. As Mbiti has pointed out, Africans traditionally regard dead relatives as members of their community as long as there is still somebody in the community alive who knew them before they died.[62] The dead person only slips away into the domain of the spirits when all those in whose memory he lived on have themselves died. For African Christians, the Bible may play this role of keeping alive the memory of Biblical characters like Abraham, Jacob and Elijah, ensuring that they never slip away. So these people are never seen in historical terms as people who lived thousands of years ago but as fellow members of the Christian faith community. The events of their lives continue to be fresh in the community's memory and the implications of those events are easily applied to the living members.

The possibility of reading one's own thoughts and agenda into the Biblical text that arises from this practice is not peculiar to it. Even in the West, after a period of optimism about the accessibility of the truth in a text, nowadays there is justifiable scepticism about it. Leslie Newbigin, in his study of the interplay between objective and subjective knowledge, observed that "all efforts to know begin with something given".[63] D S Ferguson, similarly, has pointed out that anyone trying to "hear" a text:

> inevitably hears and identifies the sounds from within a prior structure of experience or preunderstanding …None can claim an "Archimedean vantage point" from which to peer at truth.[64]

As a way of rejecting the false dichotomy between the objective and the subjective, Michael Polanyi prefers to talk about "personal knowledge", which incorporates both aspects.[65] In some quarters, especially within the philosophical movement termed postmodernism, some have become downright pessimistic, doubting that texts have objective truth in themselves, let alone truth that a reader can access.[66] All this points to the complex nature of using the Biblical text and suggests that Africans are not alone in being subjective in their use of the Bible.

What stands out about the African approach is that unlike in the West where many people are, in Polanyi's words, trusting "that we could be relieved of all personal responsibility for our beliefs by objective criteria of validity", Africans commit to the Biblical text and take responsibility for their interpretation. They do this by putting their trust in the Holy Spirit for guidance. This is understandable because the doctrine of the Holy Spirit has "the central place"[67] in the majority of African Independent Churches. The Aladura, for example, believed the Holy Spirit was the "sole authority"[68] in their church, and the Arathi, which is called "the church of the Holy Spirit", believed the whole church was "possessed" by the Holy Spirit.[69] So the Holy Spirit's direction of the church's ministry gives the leaders and the members an understanding of God's divine revelation, including revelations in the Bible.[70] This can be seen from the point of view that the inspiration of the Biblical writers and the inspired interpretation of the texts are part of the same process through which God reveals himself and other things through the Bible. What the Africans are doing is trusting in God's guidance in the process rather than leaving the responsibility for their interpretation to a method.

2.5   Conclusion

A close attachment to the Bible is one of the hallmarks of African Christianity. This close attachment, which is indicated by the frequent use of Biblical stories and references, is retained to a large extent by African Christians in Britain. This is because much of the attraction of the Bible has to do with the similarity between the worldview within it and the traditional African worldview. Because this worldview continues to survive in Africans even after many years of living in Britain, the attachment to the Bible remains very strong. However, the British social context has an influence that brings two changes. The first change occurs because the British context also gives high regard to other ways of knowing (particularly, rational argument and empirical evidence), African Christians in Britain are therefore more likely than those in Africa to support their positions with reason. Secondly, the presence of racism is leading Africans to begin to deploy the Bible in what could be seen as a political way. This is significant because, although many Africans in Africa did this in the past in their fight against colonialism (e.g., the Arathi of Kenya) and many still do so in South Africa,[71] for these particular Africans in Britain, it is the racism they are experiencing that has triggered this development. So, on the one hand, their need to integrate is driving them to adopt the epistemological traditions of their present context. But, on the other hand, their frustration at not being allowed to integrate is also affecting their use of the Bible.

CHAPTER 2 ENDNOTES

[1] Barrett: 127-134.
[2] Turner, 1965: 14–23.
[3] Turner, 1967: 83.
[4] Fashole-Luke: 135–150.
[5] Appiah Kubi and Sergio Torres ed: 192.
[6] Mbiti, 1986:42.
[7] Ibid:44.
[8] Agyin-Asare, *Power in Prayer*, 2001.
[9] *Newswatch* (Nigerian magazine) Vol. 36 No 5, Aug 5 2005.
[10] Oyedepo, *The Miracle Seed*, 1985.
[11] Agyin-Asare, *The Impact of Prayer*, 2001.
[12] Vander-Puije, 2004.
[13] Nyamu, 2000.
[14] Kiranga, 2004.
[15] Kiuna, 2003.
[16] Adeboye, 2003.
[17] Ibid.
[18] Adeboye, *Showers of Blessings*, 2003.
[19] Adeboye, 2003: iv.
[20] See Ibid: 18.
[21] See Mbiti, 1969: 15–24.
[22] Mbiti, 1986: 24.
[23] See, for example, Wilbur O'Donovan's story about a missionary called Caleb (O'Donovan's, 1996): 1.
[24] Mbiti, 1986: 24.
[25] Ibid. It is noteworthy that the history of the Anglican Church

of Kenya, as told in its official website (www.ackenya.org), is more or less synonymous with the history of the translation of the Bible into Kiswahili.

[26] Ibid: 28.

[27] Ibid.

[28] Githieya: 231.

[29] Ibid.

[30] Ibid: 234.

[31] Mbiti, 1986,32.

[32] Ashimolowo, 2003.

[33] Anyahamiwe, 2003.

[34] Odulele, A *Living by Faith*, 2003.

[35] A Odulele, *Understanding God's Voice*, 2003.

[36] Frank-Briggs, 2001.

[37] Aggrey-Solomon and Aggrey-Solomon, 2003.

[38] Odulele, *Eternity Rediscovered*, 2005: 18–19.

[39] Turner's study of this group revealed not only extensive use of the OT but that they see the Gospel from an OT perspective. See H W Turner, 1965.

[40] Githieya: 233.

[41] Tetteh is originally from Ghana, but currently ministers in London.

[42] Tetteh, *Benefits of Anointing*, 2002: 15.

[43] Odulele, *God's Voice*: 19.

[44] V Odulele, sermon at Glory House, 2/10/05.

[45] Cone, *The Spirituals and the Blues*: 81.

[46] McGrath: 158.

[47] Akanle: 15.

[48] Ibid: 16.

[49] Ibid: 160.

[50] Owolabi: 16.

[51] Kalilombe, "Race Relations in Britain: 44.
[52] Kalilombe, "My life, faith and theology": 59.
[53] Ibid: 60.
[54] Ibid: 61.
[55] Nwulu: 334.
[56] Igwara: 58.
[57] Ashimolowo, 2004.
[58] Equiano: 27–28.
[59] Cugoano: 30.
[60] Ibid: 19.
[61] See, for example, K Dickson, 1979: 166.
[62] Mbiti, 1969: 24.
[63] Newbigin: 49.
[64] Ferguson: 6.
[65] Described in Newbigin: 58.
[66] For example, the work of Michael Foucault (1926–1984) and Jacques Derrida (b.1930) described in Corrie: 7–8.
[67] Anderson: 1.
[68] Turner: 339.
[69] Githieya: 237.
[70] Daneel: 149.
[71] See for example, Mosala, 1989.

CHAPTER 3

THE DOCTRINE OF GOD

3.1 Introduction

This chapter will address how African Christians understand who God is. It will begin with a description of the understanding in Africa, and then compare that with the understanding of God by Africans in Britain to identify any differences attributable to the influence of the British context. As in the previous chapter, both the analysis of other scholars and the study of recent publications by African preachers will be used. The interviews I conducted of twenty African Christians will be used in the second part of the chapter to see what differences there may be among Africans depending on how long they have lived in Britain.

3.2 What African Christians in Africa believe about God

In his study of African Independent Churches, David Barrett found the following concepts of God: God as the Living God, the God of Power, the God of Miracles, the God of the Impossible and the God of Ancestors.[1] He also found that the leaders of these churches:

> lay the emphasis in their teaching and preaching on God as the God of the living, the God of revival and new life, the God of the impossible, the God of miracles, the God of action, the God of power, the God of the Exodus.[2]

A study by Kenneth Enang of the Annang people of Eastern Nigeria found that the operating understanding of God was one of the reasons they left the mission churches for AICs. For them,

> the God of the mission churches is a remote one, too far removed from man. Man is confronted with evils, yet He is not interested in their destiny, He does not help. He is only interested in their souls and not in their general and total welfare, bodily and spiritual.[3]

When they turn to an Independent Church, they discover a powerful God who is interested in the whole person, and the evil forces are overcome.[4]

The concept of God as Creator also features in the work of many African Christian theologians, although often in the context of the debate about the relationship between Christianity and African Traditional Religions.

African Christianity in Britain

For example, at a meeting in 1964, African theologians, collectively, stated:

> We believe that the God and Father of our Lord Jesus Christ, creator of heaven and earth, Lord of history, has been dealing with mankind at all times and in all parts of the world. It is with this conviction that we study the rich heritage of our African peoples.[5]

The Nigerian theologian, Bolaji Idowu, who holds the view that the God of the Christians is the same as the God of pre-Christian African tradition, states: "Africa recognizes only one God, Supreme, Universal God…one and the same God, Creator of all the ends of the earth."[6] Numerous names used by African Christians for God and African Christian songs also focus on God as Creator of all things.

The above findings from previous studies of African Christianity are supported by my analysis of recent writings by African Christian preachers based in Africa. These recent writings show that the "interested, powerful God" is still present in African churches. African preachers emphasize attributes or aspects of God that show God involved in their daily lives. One of the most widespread of these concepts is the tendency to see God as a provider of people's needs in this material life, including the needs for material possessions and good health. Adeboye of Redeemed Christian Fellowship makes this promise to his reader,

> Perhaps you have been blessed in the past; but today, God is poised to throw you into the ocean of His blessings. What you have received

in the past can best be described as dew. Now you are going to be drenched in God's showers of blessings.[7]

So long as one is ready to use some of this wealth to serve God, he writes, God is ready to bless you with "stupendous wealth".[8] For Oyedepo of Winners' Chapel, God's will for the believer is that the dry places of life "become as a well watered garden".[9] He pointed out that God wants to see the believer "fat" and "flourishing" in order to demonstrate his goodness in practical terms.[10] So long as one seeks God first, God will bless one with an "unlimited rain of blessings".[11]

The issue of good health is tied to this. God looks out for the Christian, catering for her needs, because God cares for the whole person. For the same reason, God is ready to heal her when she falls sick. Many African churches have an established healing ministry because they see God as a great healer. The Arathi of Kenya, from their formative years, stressed supernatural healing practices.[12] The Ghanaian preacher Agyin-Asare has a healing ministry that has taken him to different countries in Africa and even to Europe. It has been noted that the commonest reason people go to the African Independent churches is for healing.[13] Some of these churches go to the point of discouraging their members from using African or Western medication and instead promote healing through prayer to God.[14]

God's power is still commonly emphasized among African Christians. The Nigerian Preacher Akosa gives the example of God's power in the Biblical story of David and Goliath: "David knew both the scriptures and the power of God and this provided a basis for him to defeat the Philistines."[15] This power is hardly ever presented in a theoretical way, but rather in the practical sense of God's power to transform, in particular, to transform human life. It is this power that underlies God's provision and acts of healing. The Kenyan writer, David Oginde, in the book *Possessing Your Possessions,*[16] recalls how God gave victory to Joshua against massive odds in order to encourage his Christian readers that God will give them victory over their circumstances.[17] W F Kumuyi calls up the story of Ezekiel in the valley of dry bones (Eze 37), where God turned dry bones into a vast army, to show what God can do.

> If you say it exactly as the Lord wants it said, God will raise the dead. He will restore backsliders. He will heal the sick. He will sanctify believers. He will bring fire upon cold hearts. He will raise up a mighty army of believers.[18]

God's gifts, however, are not without responsibility on the part of the receiver, because God is also a judge. The Nigerian preacher, Enoch Adeboye, points out that just as God gives "showers of blessings",[19] God also can give "the flood of judgement"[20], as in the time of Noah. "The flood is meant for the ungodly while the rain of blessing has been reserved for the righteous."[21] David Oyedepo writes, similarly, about the need for repentance since, "Whenever God pronounces blessings for his people, he leaves a part for them to do."[22] The believer's actions are therefore vital because, "prosperity and good success come not just as a result of confessing the word, but DOING it."[23] Another Nigerian preacher, Olukoya, points out that to not acknowledge God is to "terminate the presence of God" in one's life,[24] a "spiritual abortion"[25] which will make God hide his face.[26]

My study of the recent work of African preachers also shows, as previous studies found, that the concept of God as Creator is important to African Christians. This concept often serves as the theological basis for what preachers say about God in relation to human beings and the world. A common view, for example, is that the God who made everything does not abandon them to their fate but sustains them by providing for and protecting them. The Kenyan preacher, Allan Kiuna writes, "We are not created to be on the losing side…winning should come easily to you."[27] Focusing on "dominion" (Gen 1:26, King James Version) as the primary reason humans were created, he assures the reader, "Whatever stands on your way to Dominion will be crushed under the feet of the Almighty."[28] It is the will of the Creator "that we may increase rapidly…Do not be afraid of asking God to help you to increase in every area of your life…Abundance beyond measure is our portion as children of God".[29] Similarly, Enoch Adeboye, reflecting on Gen 1:26, "Let us make man in our own image", stated, "God did not create any one of us to be small",[30] and "God did not create you to be just a champion. He created you to be world champion."[31] Linked to this is the idea that God has a plan for each creature, so those who accept God will see God's pre-ordained plan unfolding before them. Kiuna assures the reader, "You, yes, you are here by divine design."[32]

It is clear that these African Christian concepts of God have been influenced by the traditional African view that the spiritual and physical aspects of life are inseparable.

Enang's study showed this was why some people rejected the God of the mission churches: Whilst the mission churches made a distinction between the physical and the spiritual, the God of the Independent churches was more coherent with their supernatural view of life. This post-missionary Christian concept of God is very similar to the concept of God in African traditional religion. Studies of African traditional religion have shown that Africans see God as Creator[33], provider[34], sustainer[35], protector[36] and healer[37]. Even though a discussion of the view that the God of African traditional religion is the God of the Bible is more than can be undertaken in this space, it would appear that, at the very least, pre-Christian African concepts of God are sufficiently similar to the God of the Bible that African Christians (especially those in the Independent churches) have been able to weave the two ideas together.

3.3 The British Scene

A comparison of the writings of African Independent church preachers in Africa and their counterparts in Britain showed many similarities. The idea of God as a provider and a healer are also very common in Britain. In the sermon by Vincent Odulele of Glory House London referred to in the previous chapter, he tells his congregation:

> Let it be said that your God was able. Let it be said that he was a deliverer and a restorer on your behalf…He can fix your home and fix your business….It's over. Check it out when you get home. Go back to your doctor and say

> `run the test a second time'…Go back to your bank manager and say `give me a little time and watch'.

A similar view of God is expressed here by Matthew Ashimolowo, who has said that his special calling is to "raise champions":

> God is bringing you into your promotion because of the uncommon blessings. God is saying that there are things he has set in place, elevations, exaltations, bringing into positioning for a reason and this will break out [for all to see].[38]

God's provision is sometimes recalled in very dramatic circumstances. For example, Lawrence Tetteh of World Miracle Outreach London, recalled in his book *Count Your Blessings* how he was once stranded and while walking on the street in tears saw a fifty-pound note "lying tantalizingly on the ground in my path."[39] He also described how a pastor and his family had totally run out of food and prayed, believing "the Lord will provide".[40] As soon as they concluded the prayer, the doorbell rang. Some members of his congregation were standing outside with food — cooked meals, bread and fruits. They had come to bless the man of God. How wonderful! This is a true story of how God can indeed provide in time of need.[41]

The idea of God as a healer can be seen, for example, in the ministry and writing of the Kenyan-born Gilbert Deya, who is also based in Britain. Deya writes out specific prayers for illnesses. Here is a prayer for those suffering high blood pressure or diabetes:

> Heavenly Father, I come to you in the name of Jesus. I have been diagnosed with high blood pressure and diabetes. These are dangerous illnesses that have terminated many people's lives…High blood pressure and diabetes there is no room for you in my body. I overcome you by the blood of Jesus.[42]

Pastor Lawrence Tetteh gave this account of how God miraculously healed a man brought to the church. The man had been hospitalized for a year, but while people around him in hospital were dying, "God showed him mercy" and preserved his life.[43] Tetteh prayed for the man, and then:

> He said that he began to feel some strength in his body, so he pushed his Zimmer frame away and began to take his first unaided steps after seven years. Then he felt stronger and then began to march around full of joy and praise to God for restoring his health.[44]

As with the Africa-based preachers, God as Creator is an important concept for the British based preachers, as can be seen from this account by Tetteh:

> Over the years in my ministry, I have witnessed the amazing living reality that God is the Creator of all things. For example, a few years ago, I witnessed the creative power of God when I saw an eyeball recreated in an empty eye socket…a medically confirmed hole-in-heart case was healed without surgery. A missing tooth

grew back…kneecaps that have been surgically removed restored.[45]

There is also a clear sense that God as Creator owns everything and has power over everything. "Our lives belong to God, our families, our children and our relatives are all His. He blesses our bread and takes sickness away from us".[46] There is also the element of human participation, such as was seen among the Africa-based preachers. "God promises great blessings to his people, but many of these blessings require our active participation through meeting the conditions of his promise."[47] To "appropriate" God's blessings, the people must seek, cry out to, trust, fear and serve God.[48] They must turn from evil, do good, speak peace and be humble.[49]

Most of those I interviewed, immaterial of their denomination, country of origin and length of stay in Britain, saw God as the Creator. Other ideas that featured significantly were God as mystery, God as omnipotent, God as the owner of everything and God as the one you can trust. These resemble not only the categorizations found among African Christians in Africa, but also what has been found in African traditional religion. For example, God as Creator was found by John Mbiti to be "the commonest attribute of the works or activities of God"[50] in the pre-Christian religions of African peoples. This link and the reason behind it were observed by some of the respondents. One person said, "My ancestors who didn't know Jesus Christ, knew God. The Bible says the Spirit of God is everywhere." Another respondent gave this personal account:

> Before I became a Christian, I was aware of God. We have a name for God "Imaana" This means The Always Existing….I had no difficulty in understanding the attributes of God because it corresponded to what we believed in. The new aspect was to understand the person of Jesus Christ and the Holy Spirit.

The only discernible difference in the interview responses based on length of stay was the extent to which they thought God pre-planned everything. One respondent who has lived in Britain for about five years said:

> For me, God is not only Creator, but he is my Provider, he is my Protector. He is all things for my life. God has planned my life. Everything that happens to me has already been planned by God. That means God is all my life.

Another said he did not believe in chance. He believed that there is a Being behind the things that happen. The same point was made by a third respondent who pointed out that human beings were not in control of their destiny. In contrast, one respondent, who has lived in Britain for twenty five years, was more rational. She criticized those who think that they can totally avoid accidents by living holy lives:

> They expect that if they go to church and they tithe and they do everything right…You shouldn't be ill, you shouldn't lose your job, nothing bad must happen to you. But as an African Christian growing up in Britain, I would

understand. My understanding is that those are part of what happens in the world.

The views of those who have been in Britain for a short time resonate with Kiuna and Adeboye's idea that God made people for a purpose. On the other hand, as observed in chapter 2 in relation to changes in the worldview of Africans in Britain, it appears that British society makes Africans increasingly rational in their understanding of life events. The longer they live in Britain, the more they move away from the common African belief that physical events are usually a manifestation of spiritual realities. The same respondent put it this way: "If you step on a broken bottle, it will go through your foot regardless of whether you spent ten days sitting in church fasting and praying."[51] She also pointed out that those in Africa see Christianity as a "protective blanket"

> whereas African Christians in Britain live with everything that life throws at them and don't necessarily attribute it to God or lack of God doing something or because God did something. It's just life.[52]

The clearest sign of a Diaspora effect on the doctrine of God can be seen in the work of Africans in the "historical" (i.e., the long established) churches. For this group, there is more emphasis on God's concern for social justice. John Sentamu, writing as the Chair of the Church of England's Committee for Minority Ethnic Anglican Concern (CMEAC), points out to the Church that the gospel is about, among other things, God's justice. He quotes these words of Micah: "what does the Lord require of you but to do justice, and to love kindness and to walk humbly with your God" (Micah 6:8).[53] Contributing to another report entitled *Seeds of Hope*,[54] the Ugandan-born Sentamu suggests that racism in the structures of the Church of England might be making it difficult for them to "live up to God's vision of wholeness, freedom, order and peace".[55] The report itself points out that "the God of justice and mercy challenges his people to put right things that are wrong within the community of faith".[56]

Other historical churches have similarly expressed God's concern for social justice. Publications on racism by the Methodist Church, to which the Zimbabwean-born Naboth Muchopa is a regular contributor, point out that "a faithful God" provides among other things "words of justice, forgiveness and healing"[57] and that the church of God should focus on justice not charity.[58] The Black Catholics, also, in their Congress of 1990 stated that racism "stands opposed to every humanizing process and is contrary to God's plan for us".[59] They saw racism not as a crime but as a sin against God because how people treat one another cannot be separated from their relationship with God.[60]

These Africans also stress that God is the source of human equality. The Africans within the Roman Catholic Church (working alongside other minority ethnic people) have expressed similar ideas.

> We believe that each human being is created in the image and likeness of God; has a dignity and value that must be respected, promoted, safeguarded and defended; that we are all equal in the eyes of God; and that we are all bound together by our common humanity.[61]

They relate God not only with human equality but also with human diversity. "We believe that the ethnic and cultural diversity that has existed in Britain for centuries is a reflection of God's gift of diversity in creation"[62]; they point out that racism denies people their dignity as children of God and is contrary to God's plan for humanity.[63] Similarly, the Methodists in their resource pack on racism[64] remind participants that God makes everybody in God's own image and that God saw that his creations were good.

The theme that God is doing a new thing has also been important. John Sentamu, drawing on the picture of Ezekiel in the valley of dry bones, points out God's determination not to give up on the old establishment but rather to create a "structure that matched God's demand for a caring people he called his own".[65] This new community is one

> of interdependence pressed together by love with a wealth of variety designed to give interest and beauty and truly reflecting the characteristics of the Creator and Redeemer.[66]

The Black Catholics make a similar point, stating simply that "God is forever calling us to newness of life".[67]

In recent years, African Independent Church pastors in Britain have been reflecting God's concern for social justice. Fr Timothy Abiola of the Aladura church in Britain, out of his experience of racism in the Church of England, has asked when such a church can be regarded as "a church of God".

When somebody goes in to serve God and that person is shown another place and is told that he has come to the wrong place, then we have to find out exactly where the church of God is.

Similarly, in the sermon series *Black and Blessed*, Pastor Matthew Ashimolowo described how God moved him by the suffering and poverty of black people in London and ordained him to raise black people to be winners.[68] He urged the congregation to "refuse to be limited" and to be assured that according to the Bible, God did not count people by their colour but by their nations and families.

3.4   Issues raised by African Christians' understanding of God

One question that comes out from the African Christian understanding of God described above is whether the God of the Christian Church is the same deity worshiped in traditional African religions. This is a question that is likely to divide some of the groups that we have discussed above. As we have seen, many African theologians have no doubt about this, as was made clear by their 1964 statement. The Nigerian theologian, Bolaji Idowu, supported this by pointing out that "Africa recognizes only one God"[69]. On the other hand, apart from the first generation African Independent Churches like the Aladura and the Arathi, the ministers of African Independent Churches are likely to view such a position with suspicion. Many of them still view African religions as the sources of the many demonic spirits that they are often called to fight in their churches.

My view on this question, based on my studies of the subject and my experience, not only as an African, but having lived in Africa for many years, is that the experience of Africans when they move from traditional religion to Christianity is not one of moving form worshipping one God to worshipping another. The feeling is more of discovering a better system and structure for doing so. The experience of conversion is no less powerful for that reason. They go on to discover much more about the God they have worshipped for years, such as how much more personal and merciful God is. They discover Jesus Christ, who is God, and yet came on earth and lived among human beings. They discover the Bible, a book they can own, through which they can encounter God. They discover the Holy Spirit which can take them over and enable them to see beyond what is normally visible and to achieve beyond what is humanly possible. So even though it is the same God, they come to know that God and to enjoy that God like never before.

Another question that emerges from our description of African Christian understanding of God is to what extent is an individual's understanding influenced by church denomination? The answer to this question has many ironies. In Africa, for example, many of the theologians who advocate a merger of African Traditional Religions and Christianity come from the historical churches like the Roman Catholic, the Anglican and the Methodist. There are, however, only minor signs that all the agitation is producing changes within the life and practices of these churches. On the other hand, the new African

African Christianity in Britain

Independent Churches, who tend to be antagonistic to African Traditional Religions, are the ones who this study shows displaying significant influence by African philosophy in their understanding of Christian doctrines. The reality could be that all African denominations, both the historical churches and the AICs, are experiencing the same phenomenon. We have only detected it in the AICs because of the large number of materials published by that group of churches in recent years.

We also saw an influence in denomination in how African Christians in Britain understand God. Whist the Africans in the historical churches are beginning to treat God's stand against social injustice, seriously, the issue appears to be going unnoticed by most African Independent Churches in Britain. We do have to bear in mind that many of these churches are still quite new to Britain. It might be a matter of time before they start taking the social justice dimension of Christian theology seriously. Every Christian church has a duty to address the needs of their congregation, be they spiritual, pastoral or social. Unless they do so, they would not be seen as having a comprehensive mission to the world. As has happened in some Caribbean churches in Britain, the younger members of these African Churches may begin to see them as irrelevant to their daily life struggles and start drifting away.

3.5 Conclusion

The available evidence shows that African Christians in Africa see God as Provider, Healer and Protector. This is rooted in the belief that God is the Creator who is devoted to sustaining all of creation. These same concepts occur in African Traditional Religion. Their emphasis within African Christianity is due, at least in part, to the influence of the pre-Christian African worldview. A consideration of the evidence from Britain shows a denominational divide. Whilst the African Independent Churches in Britain show a superficial change in comparison with those in Africa, those in the historical churches are showing some evidence of a development in their understanding. As a response to racism, they are beginning to see God as having a concern for social justice and to highlight that concern publicly. They highlight the social dimensions of sin and newness. For example, the same image of "the valley of dry bones" used by the African preacher Kumuyi to proclaim God's power to save backsliders and the sick was used by Sentamu to show God's power to bring about social transformation. The change in context, however, appears to be diluting the effect of the traditional worldview on their Christian faith the longer they live in Britain. The longer African Christians live in Britain, the less likely they are to think that all events have been pre-planned by God.

CHAPTER 3 ENDNOTES

[1] Barrett: 274.

[2] Ibid: 127–130.

[3] Enang quoted in Mbiti, 1986:154.

[4] Ibid.

[5] Dickson, K quoted in Moila: 102.

[6] Idowu, quoted in Bediako, 1992: 270. See also J S Pobee: 74.

[7] Adeboye, 2003, *Showers of Blessing*: vii.

[8] Adeboye, 2003, *Divine Encounter*: 14.

[9] Oyedepo, 1997, *Showers of Blessings*: 9.

[10] Ibid.

[11] Ibid: 15.

[12] Githieya: 240.

[13] Mbiti, 1986: 75, quoting K Applah-Kubi, *Man Cares, God Heals* (New York, Friendship Press, 1981): 89.

[14] Mbiti, 1986: 75.

[15] Ozoko: 18.

[16] Oginde: 2002.

[17] Ibid: 108.

[18] Kumuyi, 2003, *ABC of Ministering Healing and Deliverance*: 23.

[19] Adeboye, 2003, *Showers of Blessings*: 7.

[20] Ibid: 8.

[21] Ibid: 8.

[22] Ibid: 44.

[23] Ibid.

[24] Olukoya, 2001, *When God Says Yes*: 19.

[25] Ibid: 9.

[26] Ibid: 19.
[27] Kiuna: 10.
[28] Ibid: 49.
[29] Ibid: 14.
[30] Adeboye, 2003, *Showers of Blessings*: 36.
[31] Ibid: 38.
[32] Kiuna: 1.
[33] Mbiti, 1970: 45.
[34] Ibid: 56.
[35] Ibid: 63.
[36] Ibid: 65.
[37] Ibid: 67–68.
[38] Ashimolowo, "Uncommon Blessing".
[39] Tetteh, 2002, *Count Your Blessings*: 27.
[40] Ibid: 29.
[41] Ibid.
[42] Deya, 2003, *Dangerous Prayers*: 82.
[43] Tetteh, 2002, *Benefits of Anointing*: 25.
[44] Ibid.
[45] Tetteh, *Benefits of Anointing*: 37–38.
[46] Tetteh, 2002, *Count Your Blessings*: 24.
[47] Ibid: 47.
[48] Ibid.
[49] Ibid.
[50] Mbiti, 1970: 45.
[51] Ibid.
[52] Ibid.
[53] *The Passing Winter*: ix.
[54] *Seeds of Hope*, 1991.
[55] Ibid.

[56] Ibid.

[57] *Strangers No More*: 8.

[58] *Resource Book* Methodist Church, Committee for Racial Justice: 4.

[59] *Congress of Black Catholics*, 1990: 2.

[60] Ibid: 1.

[61] *Racial Justice Charter*, Catholic Association for Racial Justice, 2003.

[62] Ibid.

[63] Ibid.

[64] Some of the materials in these packs do not have standard publication details.

[65] *Seeds of Hope*: x.

[66] Ibid.

[67] *Black Catholics*, Catholic Association for Racial Justice (undated publication).

[68] Ashimolowo, "What's Gone Wrong with the Man of Colour," *Black and Blessed* (undated, probably 2005).

[69] Idowu, quoted in Bediako, 1992: 270. See also J S Pobee: 74.

Chapter 4

The Doctrine of the Person of Christ

4.1 Introduction

An important question Jesus Christ asked his disciples was "who do you say that I am?" (Matt 15:16). This straightforward question has been a battleground of Christian thinking for centuries because by definition, it is at the centre of the Christian faith ("Christians" are, after all, "followers of Christ"). Over the years, the doctrine of the person of Christ has been separated into two areas; Christology (who Christ is in himself), and Soteriology (his work of salvation). This chapter will address the answers African Christians in both Africa and Britain give to Jesus's question and compare them to see what changes can be attributed to the influence of the British context.

4.2   Jesus Christ in African Christianity

In his study of the Aladura in West Africa, H W Turner found they often gave Jesus Christ a peripheral place in their doctrinal statements. Jesus's divinity was taken for granted, and his humanity was "overlooked". "He is readily absorbed in the term God, whose present manifestation in the Spirit is of more importance than his historical work in the flesh".[1] When Jesus was mentioned, Turner found that the idea of Jesus Christ as a "victorious power" was important to the Aladura.[2] John Mbiti observed the same emphasis on power not only in the Aladura churches but generally in African Christianity. Because Africans are very aware of the various powers around them, such as spirits, witchcraft, magic and the devil, the concept of Jesus as a Conqueror of the things these agents put out to trouble them (fear, anxiety, sickness, death, etc.) is important to African Christians.[3]

Jesus Christ's victory over diseases means that he is often seen as the Great Healer. Appiah-Kubi, in his study of Christology in Africa, explains that African people often attribute illness to a spiritual cause, like the breaking of a taboo, the machinations of malicious or displeased ancestral spirits, witchcraft, possession by an evil spirit or a curse by a sorcerer or an offended neighbour.[4] "Jesus Christ is thus conceived by many African Christians as the great physician, healer and victor over worldly powers *par excellence*."[5] They believe Jesus came to the world to give them life more abundantly[6] and see him as being more powerful than any evil power.[7] Hence, healing is the central activity of most AICs, and the search for it is the commonest reason people go to them.[8] These churches are encouraged by Jesus's own healing work in the Bible[9] and perform their healing "in the name of Jesus". For this reason, M L Daneel has pointed out that "an authentic African Christology should be sought in the area prepared by the traditional healer",[10] and J M Schofferleers sees the Nganga (i.e., traditional healer) paradigm as "the paradigm *per excellence*" for an African Christology.[11]

Apart from these concepts, African theologians have also come up with other ways in which Jesus might be understood, based on some traditional roles in African societies. J S Pobee and Francois Kabasele have suggested that Jesus be known as the great Ancestor. This is because Jesus Christ, like the ancestors, is "our origin";[12] he is always present, just as Bantus believe about their ancestors. Just like the ancestors who hold first place in the "mediating community" between God and humans, Jesus Christ mediates between humans and God.[13] Both Pobee and Kabasele have also written about Christ as Chief because, among other things, Jesus exercises a "sacral and priestly" function just as chiefs do.[14]. However, there is little evidence that any of these ideas have been absorbed by African Christians.

African Christian songs are another important source for the understanding of African Christologies. The significance of this is that in much of Africa, especially in the AICs, theology is still largely oral rather than written and operates by description rather than by definition.[15] To ignore songs might mean missing what has been described as the "very real Christology"[16] that exists in these churches. The dominant theme in these songs is still Jesus's victories. Here is an African Christian song from the Transvaal:

> Jesus Christ is the conqueror
>
> By his resurrection he overcame death itself
>
> By his resurrection he overcame all things
>
> He overcame magic
>
> He overcame amulets and charms
>
> He overcame the darkness of demon-possession
>
> He overcame dread
>
> When we are with him
>
> We also conquer.[17]

Another well-known African Christian song goes:

Leader:	Winner eh eh
All:	Winner
Leader:	Jesus, you are a winner
All	Winner
Leader	Battle battle you've won forever
All	Winner
Leader:	Are you a winner?
All:	I am a winner in the Lord Jesus.

These and countless other songs celebrate the power of Jesus and the victory he achieves over earthly detractors and evil forces.[18] There is also in these songs and others a clear sense in which Jesus's victory becomes that of the Christian. He conquers so "when we are with him, we also conquer", and Jesus is a winner, so "I am a winner in the Lord Jesus".

In general, African preachers write about "Jesus Christ" significantly less than they write about "God". With them, Jesus's power to save from difficult situations is also the major emphasis. The Nigerian preacher, Emmanuel Oha, writing to young people in Nigeria, promises the practical protection of Jesus Christ from marauding youth gangs attacking and intimidating the general public, "If you are determined to follow Christ, you will have shelter…Only Christ can give you comprehensive protection".[19] Similarly, Enoch Adeboye promises members of a secret, occult society that Jesus can save them from it.

> It does not matter what arrangement you made with the forces of darkness, if you come to Jesus, anything they might want to do will come to naught…Jesus is willing to deliver you, but you must be ready to take that step of faith.[20]

So, whether the threat is of a physical or supernatural nature, Jesus will deliver you. The context of a battle suggests why in these books Satan was more prevalent in connection with "Jesus" than with any other subject. For example, in a chapter entitled "Jesus loves you" in the book *Jesus Lord of the Universe*, Adeboye describes in full the story of Satan's fall from grace.[21] He warns the reader, "You must know that there is someone who wants to destroy your home, your business, and your peace. His name is Satan".[22] The Kenyan preacher, Apostle James Nganga states the case simply, "Until you know Jesus and the power embodied in him, Satan will toy around with your health."[23]

Many episodes of healing are recounted by the preachers. Adeboye tells the story of a strange incident at a church service when a boy who had been ill from birth was miraculously cured. At his birth, the boy's parents had consulted a traditional herbalist who told them to take him to Jesus Christ. When his parents refused to do this, the devil "implanted a demon to follow the child everywhere he went."[24] When the parents eventually brought the boy to meet with Jesus, he experienced a miraculous healing:

> As we were preaching, I saw a little commotion in the crowd...At the end of the sermon, I enquired after what happened and I was told that as I was preaching, suddenly a snake came out of the shirt of the child. It was when they were trying to kill the snake that I saw the commotion.[25]

Adeboye underlined the power of Jesus in this healing act by pointing out that nobody had touched the boy or prayed for him before this happened. It was just the power of Jesus working on its own.[26] The Ghanaian pastor, Agyin-Asare, whose healing ministry has taken him to many countries around the world, makes the same point:

> In our crusades, we do not shout for the sick to be healed. We hardly lay hands on the sick; we make a simple demand in the name of Jesus Christ our resurrected Lord, and it happens.[27]

African preachers also see Jesus as a Great Provider because he is a Great Problem Solver. The same way they take their diseases to him in their songs, they also take to him their lack of progress in life, such as their need to get married, have children, get a job, and get money and other material things they need to support life. Although this is a theme more linked to "God" than to "Jesus Christ", we can identify a sufficient number of cases where provision is attributed to Jesus Christ to consider this an important concept for African preachers. Emmanuel Oha in *Potential for Excellence*[28] prays against unemployment or underemployment "in Jesus name".[29] Another African preacher, Apostle Mike Ofoegbu in *Pray Down Money*[30] recommends this prayer:

> Lord Jesus, for my sake You became poor, that through Your poverty I will be rich. I enter into a covenant of prosperity with You. I will surely prosper for You have carried away my poverty and nailed it on the cross for ever.[31]

Adeboye states that "Jesus offers mansions and not one-bedroom flats",[32] "free transportation",[33] "free food and free drinks",[34] "great employment",[35] "a political post",[36] and the prospect of becoming "the most successful businessman that has ever been".[37]

The following could be noted at this point: as was observed in preceding chapters; the African worldview has left its imprints on African Christological concepts. The paucity of "Jesus Christ" in comparison to "God" observed by Turner and found in my own analysis of recent books by African preachers is probably due to the fact that Africans have always had the concept of God, whereas Jesus Christ is a new concept (as observed in the previous chapter by Malachi Munyaneza). So they naturally relate life to God more than to Jesus Christ. Also, the ever-present motif of battle and the concept of Jesus Christ as an Overcomer probably come, at least in part, from the traditional African view of the world as a spiritual theatre in which misfortune and illness are caused by evil spirits.

This coheres with Kwame Bediako's view that Africans have a "pre-Christian memory" that feeds into their "African Christian consciousness".[38] Specifically on Christology, Bediako sees the prayers and praises of a Ghanaian farmer, Afua Kuma, particularly her reference to Jesus as "the grinding stone on which we sharpen our cutlasses",[39] her references to animals and the general tone of her prayers as reflecting a feature of African primal religion,[40] which is a "fellow-feeling with nature".[41] Her reference to Jesus as "the Hunter" who goes to the deep forest to confront the evil spirit that has been troubling the village hunters draws this comment from Bediako:

> In this striking association of images, the Incarnation and the victory of the Cross are brought together and made meaningful in the defeat of the terrors of the African world

For him, the spirituality expressed by this illiterate Ghanaian woman "forms the true basis of African theology" and "provides clear evidence that Christianity in Africa is a truly African experience".[42]

4.3 The British Scene

The sermons and books by African Christians in Britain show much the same understanding of who Jesus Christ is as that described above. Just like their counterparts in Africa, those living in Britain see Jesus as their Victor (or Champion), Healer and Provider. Take, for example, the prayers recommended by Rosemary Waritay-Tulloch, an African Christian living in Britain, in her book *The Power of the Word in Your Mouth*[43] for particular circumstances. The prayers for "victory" include the following:

> The blood of Jesus is over and around my situation and I thank you for giving me the victory. I shall be like an olive tree that prospers and nothing I do will fail. Victory is mine in Jesus name.[44]

The prayer for healing acknowledges that "Christ died on the cross to take away my sickness"[45] and that "through him I am set free from the curse of the law of sickness".[46] And the prayer for "finances" acknowledges that God "owns all the silver and gold"[47] and states: "I claim my inheritance through his Son, Jesus Christ."[48] It goes on:

> Lord you have declared in your word that I am [i.e., God is] a creator of wealth. I believe that I will possess my possessions in Jesus name. I cover my wealth with the blood of Jesus and command them to locate me now in the name of Jesus.[49]

Her list of prayers includes other situations, such as children, deliverance, marriage and immigration. The point here is not that Africans are unique in using Jesus's name in prayer; rather it is that in the way the name is used that their understanding of Jesus can be discerned.

Kinsley Akoto-Bamfo, a minister in London, has written about "the power of the name of Jesus"[50] He gives the example of Peter's healing of a cripple in Act 3:6 and points out that this "supernatural power of God that has been vested in the name of Jesus"[51] is also at the fingertips of believers.[52] The name of Jesus, Akoto-Bamfo points out, "subdues every form of opposition — spiritual, physical or ethereal".[53] Another British-based African preacher, Jonathan Oloyede, preaching to the congregation of Glory House in Plaistow, London, said that whatever his listeners are going through in their lives, whatever kinds of illness they were suffering from, all they have to do is "lift up the blood of Jesus". During a period of prayer for miraculous healing, he said

> You have the victory…we command you to arise in the name of Jesus…whatever it is, we command it to submit to the lordship of Jesus…Go back to your doctor and ask him to run the check again…At the name of Jesus, that condition has bowed…Jesus is Lord. He is in control.[54]

As in the African context, the devil is often mentioned in relation to the work of Jesus. For example, Oloyede, at the beginning of his sermon warned the congregation that "The devil comes to us to steal, to kill and to destroy."[55] Another African Christian, Grace Akanle, treats the subject of Satan even more comprehensively in her book *Satan Proof Your Children*. She points out that Satan can do great harm to children. However, because of Jesus Christ, Christians are "more than conquerors"[56] because they have "overcome all kinds of evil by the blood of the lamb and by the word of our testimony".[57]

As in Africa, many songs used by African Christians in Britain are about the power of Jesus Christ. Take, for example, this song used in some African Independent Churches in Britain:

> Jesus has giv'n me victory
> I will lift him higher
> My redeemer
> I will lift him higher.

In fact, many of the songs used in Africa are used in many of the African Independent Churches in Britain.

In the twenty interviews I conducted, the commonest description of Jesus Christ were "Saviour", "Second person of the Trinity" and "Son of God". Other descriptions used were, the Way to God, a friend, He Who Was There from the Beginning and a real person. There was no difference of substance between the responses based on how long people have lived in Britain. Comparing these with the concept of Jesus in Africa, remember that the Christological concepts found among Africans in Africa were mostly Soteriological (i.e. to do with the work of Christ). There was little or nothing about who Jesus Christ is in himself. The sharp difference between this Soteriological emphasis and the emphasis on ontology among those in Britain, such as "Son of God" and "Second Person of the Trinity", probably has more to do with the way the information was derived than it does with an actual difference between the two contexts. The interviewees were responding to the simple question, "who is Jesus to you?", whereas much of the information in Africa was derived from the context of sermons and books addressing people's needs. African churches do not tend to have creedal statements. This issue will be discussed further in a later chapter. Suffice it to state here that this difference is not judged to be the result of a change in context.

One sign of change is that Jesus Christ is being associated with the fight against racism. In the Church of England report on how different dioceses were "combating racism", John Sentamu described how the cross of Jesus Christ makes all things new:

> The newness of life is not confined to personal living but radically addresses public and institutional ways of doing things. It is concerned not only with joy but also with injustice and inequality, not only with happy people of the Way, but also with a healed and restored environment.[58]

What this statement appears to be saying in the restrained language of an official Church of England document is that through the Cross, Jesus Christ is defeating not only personal sin but also institutional injustice, such as racism. Another evidence of this is in the work of the Racial Justice Unit of the Methodist Church, which is headed by the Zimbabwean-born Naboth Muchopa. In the booklet, *Making a Positive Difference*, Muchopa observes how racism affects "where we live, where we walk, where we shop, the jobs we hold and how we are educated"[59] and points out that "in workshops, schools and churches, racial divisions persist."[60] He also highlights how black and Asian people "have never had a fair chance to get ahead" and how this has led to Black and Asian people living "in extreme poverty today"[61]. Another booklet produced by the same unit urges the Methodist Church to "name racism as the evil it is"[52] and makes this point about the power of Jesus:

> To name something is to have power over it. Jesus on one occasion asked a demon "what is your name?" "Legion," came the reply. This was the first step in breaking down the power of the force that oppressed the man who was among the tombs.[63]

The implication here is that if the Methodist Church brings itself to recognize the racial injustice in its midst, Jesus Christ can in the same way break down the power of this evil.

A third example comes from the teaching of Pastor Matthew Ashimolowo of KICC. After a month-long series in which he lamented the racism black people were facing in Britain and other Western countries, he declared that Jesus Christ was the answer.

> There is a transforming power in the gospel of Jesus Christ. And it is the only source of transforming any people, any community, any individual or a group of people.[64]

This association of Jesus Christ with the political fight against racism is, however, not widespread. The open discussion of racism in churches has, until recently, happened only in the historical churches. But there is the indication that this will grow and spread as Africans put firmer roots in Britain and grow in confidence. The sermon series by Matthew Ashimolowo is particularly important in this respect. For two years running, Ashimolowo has dedicated the month of October, usually treated as Black History month by London Boroughs, to preach on the evil of racism. It is only a matter of time before firm doctrines can develop along these lines.

A different kind of change, which could also be judged to result from the influence of the British context, was detected in a survey on Christology I conducted in 2003.[65] I asked fifty Africans and fifty white European Christians the question "who is Jesus to you?" and found that their answers were not only influenced by their church denomination, but also by their ethnic/philosophical background. My analysis showed that even within the same kind of churches, Africans were more likely than white Europeans to describe Jesus Christ as "Victor", "Provider" or "Healer", and white Europeans were more likely than Africans to describe Jesus Christ as "Forgiver". I analysed the answers given by the Africans further and found that Africans who have lived in Britain longer (20+ years) were more likely to describe Jesus as "Forgiver" than those who have lived in Britain for a short time (less than 5 years), who for their part, were more likely to refer to him as "Victor".[66] In other words, the longer Africans lived in Britain, the more likely they were to see Jesus the way White British people see him. This, as I concluded, was evidence of a change in understanding due to a change in context.[67] The nature of the change is also significant. To change from "Victor" to "Forgiver" suggests a shift of focus from external and cosmic evils, with which Africans are traditionally concerned, to personal sin.

4.4 Issues raised by the doctrine of the Person of Christ

The African understanding of the person of Jesus Christ raises two important issues. The first is the possibility that this doctrine is entirely driven by the needs of Africans. Some level of influence would be understandable because of the effect of context on theology, which will be discussed later. There are dangers, however, in understanding God and Jesus Christ in a way that is dominated by people's needs. Wolfhart Pannenberg pointed out, regarding Christology, that, "Soteriology [i.e. the work of Christ] must follow from Christology, not vice versa. Otherwise, faith in salvation itself loses any real foundation."[68] If that were to happen, it would support Ludwig Feuerbach's well-known criticism that religious concepts are mere projections of human needs and wishes onto an imaginary transcendent world.[69] The consequence is that, potentially, anything can be set up as a Christology.

But this is not a danger that faces only African theology. Pannenberg's study of the relationship between soteriology (i.e. the study of Christ's work of salvation) and Christology (the study of who Christ is in himself) shows that in the history of Christology, "changes in Christological patterns have, in fact, been determined by particular Soteriological interests."[70] He found that Western Christological concepts have been influenced by human desire for salvation and deification, striving after similarity to God, duty to bring satisfaction for sins committed and, "most clearly in neo-Protestantism, projections of the idea of perfect religiosity, of perfect morality, of pure personality, or radical trust."[71] The issue, therefore, is about degree, and there is no evidence that soteriology is more influential in African Christianity than it is in other parts of the world.[72] The commonest answer given by the twenty Africans living in Britain interviewed in this study to the question, "who is Jesus Christ to you?" was "the Son of God", with "second person of the Trinity" and "Saviour" together in second place. The perception of the soteriological dominance of African theology has probably arisen because many African Christian theological concepts (including this present work) are synthesised mainly from writings in a pastoral context. The interviews showed that when a direct question is put about who Jesus Christ is, their answer is not merely soteriological. Rather they begin with who Jesus Christ is in himself, namely, "the Son of God". Although this description is different from the historical Jesus Pannenberg has in mind when he refers to "Christology", that is a matter of difference in the perception of reality between Africa and the West rather than a difference in the balance of Christology and soteriology.

The second issue arises out of the African understanding of "God" and Jesus Christ in glorious, victorious terms. To be sure, there is Biblical support for much of what they believe about God and Jesus Christ, such as Creator, Provider, Judge and Healer. God as Creator is supported by the entire Bible, particularly, Gen 1. In Ex 16, God provides manna for the people to save them from starvation, protects them against many enemies and heals those bitten by a snake with the bronze figure of snake (Num 21:9). Several Old Testament prophets also spoke of the judgment of God. Similarly, in Jesus's own ministry, he performed many acts of healing, provided food to feed thousands of his followers who were hungry (Mk 6:30–44, 8:1–10) and protected his disciples from the raging sea (Mk 4:35–41). Many parts of the New Testament present the ministry of Jesus as victory over evil, sin and sickness.[73] In the Gospels of Matthew, Mark and Luke, he rejects the temptation of the Devil to abuse his power and instead acts in the power of the Spirit.[74] In John's Gospel, he is often presented as the light that overcomes darkness and would be seen later taking on the establishment in Jerusalem.[75] In the Pauline corpus, Jesus is seen as disarming cosmic powers and authorities (Col 2:15), having power above anything visible or invisible that might separate us from him and being able in his final reign to "swallow up death in victory" (1 Cor 15:54). The early church also picked up this idea of Christ as Victor. As has been shown by Gustaf Aulen, the idea of Jesus Christ engaging in a "vicarious conflict against powers of evil" and achieving victory over them was the "dominant idea" of the Atonement in the early church and the first one thousand years of Christian history.[76]

There can be, however, an overemphasis on these physical aspects by Africans. They appear to ignore Jesus's comments on the dangers of wealth, such as "blessed are the poor…and woe to you who are rich…" (Luk 6:20–26) and his advice "don't store up treasures on earth" (Matt 6:19–20). Also, an emphasis on glory, provision, miraculous healing and material success can make this theological approach ill-prepared to deal with "failure" in these areas. For example, many African churches have theological difficulties dealing with unanswered prayer.[77] This possibly stems from the absence of serious thinking about how God is revealed in Jesus's crucifixion. Christians should always remember that God also revealed himself on the cross because the fullness of God is in Christ (Col 2:9). Knowing God as revealed through Jesus's suffering and humiliation on the cross, rather than through his glorious work in creation and history, can liberate people from the pursuit of deity-type glory and allow them to be human beings — "in God's revelation of himself in the cross, God shatters human preconceptions of divinity and human illusions about how God may be known."[78] The African drive for success is probably related to their image of a "successful" God. That way of seeing God need not be jettisoned. However, holding that in tension with the revelation of God on the cross would give a more balanced theology and help them cope better with unanswered prayer.

4.5 Conclusion

African Christians, in both Africa and Britain, see Jesus Christ as a powerful figure who is able to give them victory in all spheres of life. He is their Overcomer, their Winner and their Champion. The evidence suggests that the African pre-Christian worldview is a factor in the emphasis on power. Africans are very conscious of evil spiritual powers around them, and so a powerful spiritual figure is vital for their protection. Secondly, Jesus's power is seen as potent in all spheres of life because Africans do not separate life into the physical and the spiritual, but rather have an integrated view of reality. Based on the comparison of Independent church preachers, no change was detected in the understanding of Christ in the

Independent churches in Britain compared with those in Africa. In the historical churches, however, Jesus Christ is being conceived as caring for and having power over the social and political issues of the day. This can be seen in the work of John Sentamu of the Church of England and Naboth Muchopa of the Methodist Church. It also appears that African Christians over time begin to see Jesus Christ more as the one who forgives their personal sins and less as the one who overcomes the evil forces around them.

CHAPTER 4 ENDNOTES

[1] Turner, 1967: 344.
[2] Ibid: 347.
[3] Wessels: 110.
[4] Appiah-Kubi, "Christology": 75.
[5] Ibid: 76.
[6] Ibid.
[7] Ibid: 78.
[8] Ibid.
[9] For example, the Arathi, Githieya: 240.
[10] Ibid.
[11] Wessels: 114.
[12] Kabasele: 120.
[13] Ibid: 124.
[14] Pobee: 95.
[15] Appiah Kubi in Wessels: 108.
[16] Daneel in Wessels: 108.
[17] Wessels: 94.
[18] Ibid: 110.
[19] Oha, 2002: 75.
[20] Adeboye, 1999, *The Water and the Fire*: 23.
[21] Adeboye, 2002, *Jesus Lord of the Universe*: 24.
[22] Ibid: 47.
[23] Nganga: 29.
[24] Adeboye, 1999, *The Water and the Fire*: 30.
[25] Ibid.
[26] Ibid: 31.

[27] Agyin Asare, 2001, *Power in Prayer*: 19.
[28] Oha: 2002.
[29] Ibid: 34.
[30] Ofoegbu, 2003.
[31] Ibid: 3–4.
[32] Adeboye, 2002 *Jesus Lord of the Universe*: 31.
[33] Ibid: 32.
[34] Ibid: 34.
[35] Ibid: 35.
[36] Ibid.
[37] Ibid.
[38] Bediako, 2000: 51.
[39] Ibid: 8.
[40] Ibid.
[41] Ibid. This phrase was used by Kwesi Dickson, 1984: 48–49.
[42] Ibid.
[43] Waritay-Tulloch, *The Power of the Word*, 2001.
[44] Ibid: 28.
[45] Ibid: 14.
[46] Ibid.
[47] Ibid: 17.
[48] Ibid.
[49] Ibid.
[50] Akoto-Bamfo, 2002: 36.
[51] Ibid.
[52] Ibid.
[53] Ibid: 38.
[54] Oloyede, Sermon preached at Glory House on 2/10/15.
[55] Ibid.
[56] Akanle, 1999: 51.

[57] Ibid.

[58] Sentamu, "The Message" in *Seeds of Hope*: ix.

[59] Muchopa: 5.

[60] Ibid.

[61] Ibid: 11.

[62] *Beyond Duty*: 5.

[63] Ibid.

[64] Ashimolowo, "The Coming Great Transformation", *Black and Blessed,* 2004.

[65] Chike, 2003 (unpublished BA Dissertation, University of Gloucestershire).

[66] Chike: 26.

[67] Ibid: 28.

[68] Pannenberg: 48.

[69] Ibid: 47.

[70] Ibid.

[71] Ibid.

[72] See also Oduyoye, *African Theology en Route*: 115.

[73] Greene: 17–3.

[74] Ibid.

[75] Ibid: 17–4.

[76] Aulen: 22.

[77] For example, the Aladura (Turner, 1967: 367)

[78] Bauckham: 182.

Chapter 5

The Doctrine of Salvation

5.1 Introduction

This chapter will be devoted to how salvation is understood in African Christianity. The first task will be to describe how salvation is understood on the African continent. This will be followed and compared with the understanding of salvation among African Christians in Britain. As in previous chapters, the comparison will be based on material from a variety of sources, but most particularly the work of AIC preachers.

5.2 Salvation for African Christians in Africa

Once again, Turner's study of the Aladura in the 1960s is a good starting point. He found in the Aladura an "enlargement" in the scope of salvation compared to his own Western understanding. The church's statement was of a salvation that embraced the "health of body and soul, the obtaining of goodness and the weal of mankind in all matters or things temporal as well as spiritual".[1] He notes that by this understanding, the Aladura extended salvation from the spiritual to the temporal and material spheres, thereby "manifesting the divine victory not only over human but over the super human and the cosmic."[2] He noted, for example, that unlike in the West, their testimonies were about vital things like life and security, calamities avoided, rescues from evil and practical successes.[3] He gave the example of one report of a "spiritual revival" that said, "The outcome was splendid. Souls were won…many were healed…and in an interview with the Estate Housing Committee a house was allocated to him".[4]

Kenneth Enang, in his study of the understanding of salvation among the Annang people of Eastern Nigeria in 1979, identified that they understood salvation in the following ways. 1) Salvation means first deliverance.[5] Statements from the church leaders during interviews include, "Salvation is deliverance from the power of evil principalities and the enclaves of human enemies";[6] "salvation is liberation of man from the powers of the demon",[7] "the defeat of evil entities and the wicked plans of the enemy",[8] "deliverance from the traps of evil beings",[9] and "deliverance from ill health and misfortune".[10] 2) Salvation is wholeness, being in peace — "where one is in unity with himself, with his neighbours, friends and God, he can say that he is in salvation".[11] 3) Salvation is progress in life, "good health",[12] "flourishing economic concerns"[13] and "having children."[14]

African Christianity in Britain

The Kenyan theologian John Mbiti has also noted that African Christians, especially those in the Independent churches, have broadened the understanding of salvation beyond simply the question of sin and soul (as the missionaries present it) to include a physical deliverance.[15] On deliverance, Kofi Appiah-Kubi writes, "There is more than ample evidence to show that the main preoccupation of many African Christians is redemption from physical dilemmas or evil forces."[16] On material possessions, Cyril Okorocha's story about his encounter with a Nigerian business woman provides further evidence. He asked her whether she was saved:

> "O yes," she replied and then proceeded to narrate how in fifteen years in the long distance haulage business none of her vehicles had ever been involved in a road accident. Furthermore, she was very wealthy, had several houses in town and above all had two grandsons and a third was on the way.[17]

The emphasis on deliverance from distress in the present life and blessings in this world are, according to these studies, a common feature of the African understanding of salvation.

African preachers rarely use "salvation" or "saved". When they use "salvation" or one of its related words, it is often in the strict sense of conversion to Christianity. The Kenyan preacher Pius Muiru described how on the night of his conversion, a voice told him repeatedly at night to "give his life to Jesus". Later in the morning, he looked up six other people known to him "to pray for my salvation".[18] Another Kenyan preacher, Apostle

James Nganga, writing about his own conversion, stated: "When I was delivered my life changed. God started manifesting himself in different ways. He established my life. From a common beggar to a comfortable life."[19] Very often, salvation is linked to its benefits. Adeboye writes, "The moment you give your life to Jesus Christ, God deposits a seed of greatness in you. From that moment he expects you to end up at the top."[20] The predicament of the "unsaved" is the opposite: "While God's children are busy enjoying the blessings, the unsaved are suffering in the flood of destruction."[21] Pastor Robert Kayanja, founder and senior pastor of Miracle Centre Cathedral in Kampala, Uganda, makes this link between what Christ has done and its benefit to the Christian:

> The Salvation of the Lord is the price for your breakthrough. The Lordship of Christ is the ability of God to deliver you and make you successful. Jesus took our illness, sickness, infirmity, diseases…He took our place. He overcame them all. And because he won, we win.

Word study alone, however, would not give the full understanding of the concept of salvation. Cyril Okorocha, who has studied this concept in his Igbo tradition and in Christianity, has pointed out that for Africans "every religious quest is a quest for salvation and the central theme of African religiosity is salvation."[22] The question, "what for African people is salvation?" therefore amounts to "what are African people seeking from God?" or, for the preachers, "what are they offering people in the name of God?" Some of the material already presented answers these questions. Agyin-Asare, the Ghanaian, stated that people get healed when they make a demand in the name of Jesus Christ "our resurrected Lord". Mike Ofoegbu described how Jesus could enter into a "covenant of prosperity" with the believer by carrying away the believer's poverty and "nailing it on the cross for ever".

Further study of the work of African preachers shows that overwhelmingly, what Africans are seeking from God are protection, healing and provision. For example, D K Olukoya, who often discusses the divine battle with the Evil One, writes in *The Lord Is a Man of War*, "He can decide to daze your enemies or he can simply decide to inject them with a very deadly 'anaesthesia' just to clear them off the way."[23] Mike Ofoegbu in *Family Liberation Prayers* lists the following problems that constitute "Satanic harassment"[24] for the families concerned: rising and falling in status, lateness in marriage, miscarriage and barrenness, mysterious deaths, divorce and re-marriage, poverty, strange sickness, not having a male heir, a lack of peace of mind, idol-worshipping ancestors and polygamous family difficulties.[25] He urged readers to pray to God regarding the one relevant to them and promised that "God will surely liberate your family in Jesus's name."[26]

There is here a strong influence of traditional African thinking. Unlike in the West, where guilt is the main issue,[27] the issue for African Christians is the battle for life against the many dangers they see in their world.[28] So the threats are not so much within as without. Concern about sin is, primarily, not for the avoidance of guilt or the pursuit of heaven, but rather because it could hinder harmony with God and deny them God's protection and provision. The lack of emphasis on eternal life is probably because they have an integrated view of the world, making no distinction between physical life and spiritual life. Prayers in African traditional religion tend to be for life, wealth, childbearing, good health, longevity, and so on[29] — the same things that concern African Christians.

Turner reached similar conclusions in his study of the Aladura. He pointed out their awareness that there is more evil than can be attributed to human nature and that "a demonic domain of principalities and powers stands ranged against both God and man, [which] leads to a cosmic conception of evil".[30] This, in turn, "demands a cosmic view of Christ through whom this deliverance is effected"[31] and "a total view of salvation".[32] Similarly, Mbiti, who has studied the subject more widely, identifies the African worldview as one of two "strong" influences in the African understanding of salvation (the other being the Bible).

> This traditional world plays a major part in people's hearing, understanding, experiencing and application of biblical salvation. This biblical salvation comes where people are, and they open the doors of their world to it. It is inevitable, therefore, that this traditional background colours the way salvation is interpreted and applied.[33]

5.3 The British Scene

Cyril Okorocha's statement that "for African peoples, every religious quest is a quest for salvation"[34] is helpful in the consideration of what salvation is for African Christians living in Britain. Rather than asking how these British-based Africans use the word "salvation", the question is, what are they looking to God for? The answer is that in part, at least, they want the very same things African Christians in Africa are looking for — victory over human and spiritual detractors, good health, prosperity and general wellbeing. There is some evidence of this in the material already examined. For example, Vincent Odulele described God as "a deliverer" and "a restorer" because he can "fix your home and your business". And because God is a deliverer, he has healed the sick members of the congregation, so "go back to your doctor and say 'run the test a second time'". For Gilbert Deya, the blood of Jesus "overcomes" high blood pressure, and for Rosemary Waritay-Tulloch, the same blood of Jesus gives prosperity. I pointed out a similar connection in the African Christian song, "Jesus has given me victory…My Redeemer", and my survey in 2003 also showed that for African Christians in Britain, Jesus's saving work is experienced as provision, healing and victorious deliverance from illness and evil forces.[35]

In *Dangerous Prayers to Break Satan's Forces*,[36] Gilbert Deya, the Kenyan-born preacher, writes specific prayers for "sending evil spirits back to the sender",[37] "destroying thousands of enemies around you",[38] "when the spirits of death is surrounding you",[39] "when you are around wicked people",[40] "nine prayers against secret plans of the devil",[41] and "releasing punishment to those who want to kill you".[42] K J Akoto-Bamfo, who is based in Britain, writes in *Breaking the Power of Despair*:

> I want to assure you that God has programmed you for success. It's not his intention that you should be in the cave. Leave the cave of despair, financial and spiritual difficulty, family problems and societal problems.[43]

This does not mean these African preachers ignore the promise of eternity. In *Eternity Unveiled*,[44] Albert Odulele described how, on a plane journey in 2004, he was taken out of his body by an angel of God to a place where he experienced "the reality of eternity".[45] From the experience, he noted:

> The gospel is in danger of raising believers who are perfectly suited for the world but unprepared for eternity. We have learnt the principles of faith for health, wealth, wellbeing, family, success, etc. but have largely left out the purpose for these things. [46]

He warned his readers to avoid living for the "things of men" (a reference to Matt 16:23–24), and denounced what he termed the "prosperity of fools" (i.e., like the rich man in Luk 12:16–21). Lawrence Tetteh sounded the same note in *Count Your Blessings*. He warned those who might trust in their money that "even though wealth is a defence, we must remember that money cannot buy everything…You can have all the wealth in the world but without salvation, your life has no substance."[47]

As observed in previous chapters, alongside signs of continuity, there are signs of change that can be attributed to the effect of the British context. For example, in an article entitled "Seeking Health with Faith or No Faith", Bernard Nwulu, an African Christian living in Britain, looks from a Christian point of view at how the British National Health Service is failing black people. He points out that

> the goal of Christian mission is not merely an individual, personal, spiritual salvation but also the realization of the hope of justice, the socializing of humanity and peace for all creation.[48]

Nwulu laments that in the context of psychiatric provision, this justice aspect of salvation "is not evident for all people".[49] Black people were more likely to be removed by the police under section 136 of the Mental Health Act, more likely to be detained in Hospital under Sections 2, 3 and 4, more likely to be diagnosed as suffering from schizophrenia or other forms of psychotic illness, more likely to be detained in locked wards in psychiatric hospitals and given high doses of medication, less likely to receive "appropriate and acceptable" diagnoses or treatment at an early stage and less likely to be offered psychotherapy or counselling.[50] Even when the nature of the illness and frequency of contact with service providers is similar between ethnic groups, "something goes wrong for black people relative to others."[51] Nwulu advocates a liberation theology approach to tackling this racism in the provision of health care. This involves "internal liberation" in the form of helping people change their self image and "external liberation" in the form of committing to social justice and taking risks "to alter oppressive structures".[52] This, Nwulu explains, would be conforming to the pattern set by Jesus Christ:

> We need to remember that the Saviour came not for the sake of the righteous, but for sinners;

not for the sake of the healthy but for the sick (Mk 2:17).

So Nwulu's understanding of salvation goes beyond the individual to include the socio-political. He addresses the oppression of black people as a people and argues that helping black people get a better self image and opposing the "oppressive structures" holding them down is a continuation of the saving work of Jesus Christ.

Further evidence of this way of understanding salvation come from the reflections of the black theologian Emmanuel Lartey following the racist killing of black teenager Stephen Lawrence and the "institutional racism" that characterized the investigation by the Metropolitan Police. Lartey, who was from Ghana but was living in Britain at the time, began by pointing out that what happened to Stephen Lawrence and the way it was handled by the police was not new to black people: "Black folk live these realities on a daily basis and have done so for many years."[53] However, any racial attack is a theological matter. It is in effect an attack against God[54] because

> God in his infinite and inscrutable wisdom created human persons with different skin hues…God created humanity in diversity and variety. None of us has a choice as to what our birth place, heritage, culture or skin colour will be. It lies within the providence of God.[55]

Similarly, any discrimination or oppression of black people because they are black is an affront to the Creator:

> Every attempt historically to force any human persons to be in essence or existence other than they are, as created by God, is a heinous sin against God who in his wisdom created all.[56]

And any denial by black people themselves of their colour, heritage or language, perhaps due to internalisation of negative stereotypes of blackness or in order to become "acceptable" to white people, is wrong in God's eyes.

> To refuse to be what we are, as created by God, is a denial of God the Creator and a rejection of a loving relationship with God…This is a reflection of the alienation from creation and Creator that is a source of much black self-hatred.[57]

Lartey's central point is summed up in these words: "God created us 'different'. We must affirm our difference. It is necessary to recognize that such 'otherness' (difference) is crucial in the theological quest."[58] In other words, an important part of what black people in Britain are seeking from God is the freedom to be black. By implication, salvation is overcoming all the forces, internal and external, that make this difficult. Hence, there is in Lartey's views (although he has not spelled it out) a view of salvation in a socio-political sense, such as was observed with Nwulu.

A third contribution is one that can be discerned from the sermons of Matthew Ashimolowo. Ashimolowo's contribution is particularly important because it shows that what has so far been discussed in academic journals is now being preached openly in an African Independent Church. Like Lartey, Ashimolowo did not set out to articulate a doctrine of salvation. However, it is possible to discern some aspects of one from his sermon series, *Black and Blessed*.[59] In a sermon entitled "what's gone wrong with the man of colour", he traces the problem of black people to Biblical times, to idol worshipping and turning away from God. In spite of warnings by the prophets Isaiah, Jeremiah and Ezekiel, black people, who he claims are represented in the Old Testament as "Egypt", did not listen. God scattered them from their original land and punished them with disunity, slavery and foolishness. Their salvation, Ashimolowo points out, lies in turning back to God in repentance, and this would lead to a restoration of their fortunes as a people. Although Ashimolowo's analysis could be seen as over-reliant on the Bible for history, it is a serious attempt to look at black people as a group. He also shows evidence of recognizing a social dimension of salvation, although he still roots it in a spiritual problem and leaves the response in the hands of black people themselves.

The interviews I conducted with twenty African Christians in Britain also confirm that this change is happening. Asked what in their experience African Christians were seeking from God, respondents included, "survival", "someone to help", "money", "mortgage", "material things", ""salvation", "kingdom of God", "everything", "eternal life", "purpose of existence", "protection", "the miraculous", "fulfilment in life", "leadership", "provision", "empowerment", "acceptance" and "guidance". Taken together, these answers show that these African Christians, like their counterparts in Africa, do not make a distinction between the physical and spiritual aspects of life. When some explained the nature of the relationship between salvation/kingdom of

God and earthly blessings, it was similar to the situation in the African context. One person said:

> The Bible says seek ye first the kingdom of God and his righteousness and every other thing will be added onto it. So I will say that they are seeking first the kingdom of God. Somebody like me I know that if I worship and serve God it is my own belief as an African that whatever it is that I am looking for God will provide it.

A comparison of the answers based on length of stay showed that African Christians who have lived in Britain for a long period were more likely to bring a social justice dimension into their response. One respondent, who is a black Catholic, said: "In Britain, African Christians are in bondage because of issues to do with institutional racism and discrimination and lack of opportunity." Another explained that African Christians in Britain depend on God for all manner of things, and for them the church has become:

> that community that helps us through God, through the people of God to cope with the pressures of racism, unemployment, inequality and other issues that affect us as Africans in Britain.

Another respondent, who has roots in Nigeria but has lived in Britain for more than twenty years, said:

> Christian Africans in Britain are looking for God to uphold us in the land of the stranger. In terms of making a breakthrough in work, studies, to reach places that we have never reached before;

in being able to get to and get through the glass ceiling that has been created due to barriers of culture, barriers of skin colour, barriers of sex as well.

"Acceptance" and "acknowledgment" featured in a number of responses. One respondent, who comes originally from Ghana but has lived here for many years, spoke of the challenges of living in Britain in Biblical terms:

> I believe that African Christians in this community, their expectation is of a God who would take them out of Egypt, like the Israelites, in terms of their status in this country in terms of breaking through.

She described her own personal experience of being discriminated against. The need was for breakthrough "in the area of accepting us as black people with intelligence and qualifications," and to be "acknowledged for what we are and what we are able to do to get the reward that we deserve."

5.4 Issues raised by the doctrines of salvation

The key feature of the African Christian understanding of salvation is its all embracing nature. Turner, a Westerner, rightly rejects simply seeing this as "materialism" because it is usually accompanied by a strong sense of a spiritual world.[60] It is rather "an integrated view of life" in which "nature, man, and the spiritual world form a total community"[61] and where people seek a peaceful relationship with every aspect of life and expect success to be manifest on the physical level of wealth, physical strength, happy marriage, numerous children, etc.[62] This is similar to the Old Testament idea of *shalom*, which encompasses the idea of peace, wellbeing and prosperity, and with which God blesses those he favours (e.g., Lev 26:6ff). Everywhere in the Old Testament, peace and prosperity are seen as God's reward to those whose ways are pleasing to him. For example, Pr 16:7, "When a man's ways are pleasing to the Lord, he makes even his enemies live at peace with him." And Ps 128:1–2, "Blessed are all who fear the Lord, who walk in his ways. You will eat the fruit of your labour; blessings and prosperity will be yours." Where "salvation" or "saved" is used in the Old Testament, it is in a "quite concrete" sense that "covers more than spiritual blessings,"[63] such as deliverance from earthly enemies (Ex 15:2, Ps 3:8), wellbeing (Deut 32:15, Ps 85:9) and "the effect of God's goodness on his people" (Ps 53:6).

This sense of an all-embracing salvation is retained in the New Testament, even though the more spiritual aspect of forgiveness of sin receives a stronger emphasis. Crucially, Jesus's own words show this wider sense. In Luk 7:50, Jesus says to the "sinful woman" regarding forgiveness of her sins, "Your faith has saved you", and Mk 10:52 uses the same Greek word for the blind man to imply restoration of sight. In Mk 5:28, he uses "saved" with a double meaning when he told the woman who had been suffering from bleeding, "Daughter, your faith has healed you, go in peace and be freed from your suffering." Kenneth Barker observes, "Here both physical healing ('be freed from your suffering') and spiritual salvation ('go in peace') are meant."[64] This suggests that, in the way he used the word, Jesus did not make a distinction between physical and spiritual salvation.

Different Christian peoples around the world are also declaring their understanding of salvation in broad terms. The World Council of Churches in Bangkok in 1973 affirmed that salvation was "of the soul and the body of individuals and society, humankind and the 'groaning of creation' (Rom 8:19)"[65] and included in its examples, "peace of the people in Vietnam, Independence in Angola and justice and reconciliation in Northern Ireland."[66]

Problems arise when some African preachers totally ignore the spiritual dimension of salvation regarding the forgiveness of sin with the goal of eternal life with God. In many cases, salvation is presented as though it is all about material blessings. This has led to the charge of "Prosperity Gospel" (i.e., the reduction of the gospel message to the promise of material prosperity). Although many people who make this charge would not know much about the philosophical root of that emphasis in the African worldview, and it is by no means a charge that can be made of all African preachers, it is a charge that has substance and implies serious dangers. The first is the danger of an over-realised eschatology, the possibility that the consummation to which the Christian looks forward is expected in the present and the "essential eschatological perspective of faith is lost."[67] This would be disastrous because the transformative and sustaining power of the hope for the coming reign of God for both individual faith and the church's life would be lost. As Gutierrez has pointed out, confidence in the future is vital for a "commitment to the creation of a just society"[68] in the present. And regarding the Church, Hans Kung has rightly warned that a church that forgets that itself and its time are temporary "makes too many demands upon itself; it grows tired and weak and will fail because it has no future."[69]

Secondly, the African understanding of salvation can reduce the seriousness with which sin is treated. Cyril Okorocha found that two Nigerian Christians he spoke to saw their salvation in terms of prosperity and triumph over their enemies, but said little about their personal sin. Where sin is considered in this approach, it is often as a possible barrier to blessing. This limited understanding does not reflect the seriousness with which sin is treated in the NT and may not be the sufficient deterrent needed for building a just, moral society. What is needed is a balance between the concern for material needs and eternal life. In Britain, Albert Odulele's *Eternity Unveiled*, written after he came back to life from the experience of dying and in which he echoes Jesus's message in Mat 6:20–21 ("don't store up treasures on earth")[70] is a step in that direction.

5.5 Conclusion

Africans see salvation in a way that covers the whole person. Examples include deliverance from the power of evil; being at peace with one's self, neighbours, environment and God; progress in life; good health; having children and getting the material things one needs. Sometimes, the word "salvation" itself is used to mean conversion and given the connotation of something that should precede these blessings (or breakthrough). This African understanding has been influenced by the

African worldview. Salvation for them covers all spheres of life because they have an integrated view of the world, and it focuses on overcoming dangers because they see evil powers ranged against them. The analysis of the work of British-based African preachers shows that most have retained this understanding with very little change. Interviews with African Christians in Britain and other available material, however, show a changing understanding attributable to the British social context. Racism in Britain is prompting British-based African Christians to understand what they are seeking from God in social justice terms, such as desiring acceptance in Britain and the breakdown of racist barriers.

CHAPTER 5 ENDNOTES

[1] Turner: 365.
[2] Ibid: 366.
[3] Ibid: 358.
[4] Ibid: 357.
[5] Mbiti, 1986: 152.
[6] Ibid.
[7] Ibid.
[8] Ibid.
[9] Ibid.
[10] Ibid.
[11] Ibid.
[12] Ibid.
[13] Ibid.
[14] Ibid.
[15] Mbiti, 1986: 156.
[16] Appiah-Kubi "Christology": 72.
[17] Okorocha: 63.
[18] Muiru: 10.
[19] Nganga: 18.
[20] Adeboye, 2003, *Showers of Blessings*: 38.
[21] Ibid: 8.
[22] Okorocha: 60,
[23] Olukoya, 2001, *The Lord Is a Man of War*: 13.
[24] Ofoegbu, 2000: vi.
[25] Ibid: iv.
[26] Ibid: 2.

[27] Turner, in Okorocha: 62.

[28] Mbiti, 1986: 156.

[29] Okorocha: 68–69.

[30] Turner: 365.

[31] Ibid.

[32] Ibid.

[33] Mbiti, 1986: 156.

[34] Okorocha: 60.

[35] Chike.

[36] Deya, 2003.

[37] Ibid: v.

[38] Ibid.

[39] Ibid.

[40] Ibid.

[41] Ibid.

[42] Ibid.

[43] Akoto-Bamfo: 54.

[44] Odulele: 2005.

[45] Ibid: 33.

[46] Ibid: 52.

[47] Tetteh, 2002, *Count Your Blessings*: 25.

[48] Nwulu: 233.

[49] Ibid.

[50] Department of Health Report of the Commission Inquiry into Complaints about Asworth hospital (2 vols; London: HMSO, 1992) quoted in Nwulu: 233.

[51] N Goater *et al.*, "Ethnicity and Outcomes of Psychosis", British Journal of Psychiatry 175 (1999), p34–42, quoted in Nwulu: 233.

[52] Nwulu: 235.

[53] Lartey: 79.

[54] Ibid: 80.
[55] Ibid.
[56] Ibid: 83.
[57] Ibid.
[58] Lartey: 83.
[59] Matthew Ashimolowo Media Ministries, 2005
[60] Turner, 1967: 356.
[61] Ibid: 357.
[62] Ibid.
[63] Marshall: 610.
[64] Barker in Pradis Software.
[65] *Bangkok Assembly*: 88.
[66] Ibid: 90.
[67] Ibid.
[68] Gutierrez, 1996: 197.
[69] Kung: 97.
[70] Odulele, 2005:78–79.

CHAPTER 6

THEOLOGICAL ISSUES RAISED

6.1 Introduction

The discussion so far raises a number of Biblical and theological questions. The following will be discussed in this chapter. 1) Is it right for Africans to incorporate their African worldview into their Christian ideas? 2) Should they be allowing their Christian thinking to change due to the change in context? 3) Have they got right the balance between the Bible and other sources of Christian theology? 4) Have they allowed soteriological concerns to dominate their doctrines of God and Christ? 5) Does their conception of God in very glorious terms have harmful limitations? 6) What are the strengths and weaknesses of understanding Christian salvation in such a broad way?

6.2 The incorporation of an African worldview in their Christian thought

The question could be asked of African Christianity, whether, in view of the extent to which its Christian ideas are woven with its pre-Christian worldview, it is still authentically Christian. Is not what is required of every Christian (at least as an aspiration) pure Christian thinking, untainted by non-Christian ideas? The trouble with this line of thinking is that, even if such "pure Christian thinking" were desirable, it might not be achievable. Insights from epistemology and the sociology of knowledge should make one sceptical about this. For example, R J Middleton and B J Walsh, who write about epistemology, acknowledge that "the world has a givenness that is ontologically prior to our knowing";[1] nonetheless, they point out that the only way that we can know the world is "via our representation of the world, our worldview, our perspective."[2] They would dismiss any denial of the interference of one's worldview in the process of knowing as "naïve realism". Such denial, far from being an idle delusion, however, could become the source of oppressive behaviour. As Karl Mannheim has observed, those who refuse to accept that their knowledge is rooted in their social situation and believe instead that they have found an absolute tend to be the same people who see themselves as superior to other people.[3]

Evidence from other regions of the world also supports the position that Christianity is inextricably linked to the prevalent worldview. This is becoming more noticeable as more non-Westerners discard the Western mentality with which Christianity was packaged when it was brought to them. In Latin America, liberation theology emerged in the late 1960s as their indigenous theologians developed sufficient confidence to search out their own answers to their own questions. Whilst their search has been prompted in part by deprivation, their methods have been hugely influenced by the Latin American worldview. P Casaldaliga and J Vigil pointed out how, in that region, the spiritual and the physical are woven together.

> The Spirit and "spirits" form part of the cosmovision of mythology and daily life: birth and death, husbandry and harvest, travels…all have their palpable blessings and curses. The most immediate and spontaneous explanation is always supernatural, "mythical."[4]

Hence, Latin American spirituality is characterized by constant reference to actual conditions[5] and "the more conscientiously we live and act the more spiritual we are."[6] This worldview sees spiritual, economic and political problems as integrated and explains why many of their Christian theologians are so politically active.

A similar process is going on in Asia. The Christian writer Masao Takenaka, who writes from the Japanese context, states:

> In Asia, we are only beginning to seek, with conscious effort, to be Japanese Christians in a Japanese cultural context, Indian Christians in an Indian cultural context, and Chinese Christians in a Chinese cultural context.[7]

The Korean Christian theologian Jung Young Lee sees much of the problem with Christian theology as arising out of the either/or of the Western worldview.[8]   He recommends a Chinese worldview that has a both/and approach expressed in the interplay of *yin* and *yang*.[9] In *yin and yang*, (i.e., male and female, or active and passive) the emphasis is on complementarity not on conflict. As an approach, it would, for example, prevent a situation in which the continuity between God's creative work and God's saving work is ignored.[10] It is also particularly helpful in Christology.

> Jesus as the Christ as both God and man cannot really be understood in terms of either/or. How can man also be God? However, in *yin yang* terms, he can be thought of as being both God and man at the same time.[11]

The West, also, has experienced and continues to experience the link between Christian ideas and the prevailing worldview in its society. For example, Western understanding of atonement has tended to shadow what it sees as the basic human predicament.[12] In the twelfth century, after a great revolution of feeling in Europe, the human predicament was seen as a loss of love, and the cross was seen in terms of "turning human hearts back to love."[13] Political and social upheaval in the Reformation period (fourteenth to seventeenth century) led to an understanding of humans as "law breakers" and Atonement as paying the penalty for a crime.[14] In the Enlightenment, when there was much confidence in human reason and suspicion about religious experience, the human predicament was seen as falling short of an ethical standard and Atonement was understood in terms of changing the human being rather than the "placating of any supernatural authorities"[15] In fact, the Western worldview still retains the effect of the Enlightenment, and this continues to influence Christian thinking. There is still widespread scepticism about miracles among Western Christians; morality is still for many people the central point of religion; rationality is still given priority by many in Christian circles, and the natural and human sciences, highly regarded in Western societies, continue to be adopted into theological analysis, as can be seen from the way Western discussions of the doctrine of the Trinity often draw from the fields of psychotherapy and sociology.[16]

The issue from the foregoing becomes that of equality; that is, are not Africans entitled to do what Christians from other regions are doing, which is relating with the Christian religion from their existing worldview? The grain of the Biblical message suggests that all human beings, intrinsically, are equal in God's eyes no matter where they come from. Rom 3:23, "all have sinned and fall short of the glory of God", shows the depraved state of all human beings before God; and John 3:16 states that God's salvation is available to all — to whoever believes in Christ; all have a common humanity with the Incarnate Son, and, among Christians, all are members of his body (1 Cor 12:14–26), each having a valuable contribution to make. The doctrine of the Trinity has also been argued as providing a good ground for maintaining that all human beings are equal.[17]

> Theologically and historically the Trinity has been held to function as a model of persons-in-relationship. In this social model, Father, Son and Spirit are co-equal in status and exist in a

relationship of dialogue, reciprocity, self-giving and mutual love.[18]

Because, according to Gen 1:26–27, the image of God was given to "human beings in plural form",[19] human persons could be considered equal to each other just as the "persons" of the Trinity are co-equal.

6.3 The change in Christian thinking due to change in context

In the preceding chapters, the British social context could be seen affecting African Christians in two ways. Firstly, it was making them more rational in their outlook to the world, seen, for example in the greater use of non-Biblical material by their pastors and the mentality, as one person put it, that "If you step on a broken bottle, it will go through your foot regardless of whether you spent ten days sitting in church fasting and praying." Secondly, the presence of racism was making them more conscious of social-justice concerns. For example, they show a greater awareness of the social justice concerns of God and see salvation in social terms. But should social context, which could change from time to time, determine how God is known? Does this not leave the doctrine of God and other Christian doctrines at the mercy of the prevailing social fashion or concern?

In answer to such questions, it could be pointed out that human experience has been taken seriously as a source of theology within Christianity since the 19th century.[20] In the past fifty years, at least, this has come to be understood not just as "religious experience" but as the concrete, daily experience of life. Evidence of this can be seen in the field of practical theology which has been defined by its practitioners as "where contemporary experience and the resources of the religious tradition meet in a critical dialogue that is mutually transforming"[21] and where "pastoral experience serves as a context for the critical development of theological understanding".[22] To most practical theologians, the Christian tradition is not set in stone. It can be reshaped with experience gained from real life situations through a rigorous process of reflection. This tradition is also well established in the theologies of liberation. As a response to the poverty around them, Latin American theologians emphasise God's special care for the poor and take the reality of a poor person as the point of departure in the theological process.[23] African American theologians take the same attitude towards the experience of their people. In the words of James Cone:

> There is no truth for and about black people that does not emerge out of the context of their experience…This means that there can be no Black Theology which does not take the black experience as a source for its theology.[24]

The Incarnation provides doctrinal justification for theology that develops in response to social context. What would be behind such objections is a dualistic cosmology that sees God and the spiritual world as apart and in opposition to the material world.[25] This is not a Christian understanding, because in the Incarnation, God the Son took flesh and lived among human beings. As Gutierrez has pointed out, this was the culmination of "the oldest and most enduring Biblical promises",[26] which were the "active presence of God in the midst of his people".[27] For example, "I shall dwell in the midst of the Israelites" (Ex 29:45), and "they shall live under the shelter of my dwelling" (Eze 37:27). The language of "dwelling" (*shekinah*) is itself significant because it is about "presence in a particular place", and it "characterizes the type of relationship between God and human beings."[28] So a theological approach that is responsive to its environment is really following the model set by God.

Some sociologists have, in fact, argued that such a phenomenon is inevitable. The theologian/sociologist Robin Gill, for example, has described how theological position can be influenced by socio-cultural, socio-political and socio-ecclesiastical factors. He argued, for instance, that talk of secularisaton had "a very real influence" on the theology of the 1960s.[29] Another well-known example has been given by Pattison and Woodward. They write:

> A revision of Christian views of God occurred in the aftermath of the Holocaust when it became apparent that understandings of the nature of God needed to be changed in the face of the reality of experience of unimaginable mass suffering.[30]

These issues are similar to the issues encountered regarding worldview, which makes sense because the deep-seated philosophical view of the world and knowledge gained through life experience in a specific context are part of the pre-understanding people bring to their interpretation of reality.[31] The same issue of equality arises. Africans, like other people, should have the benefits of a Christian faith that is rooted and responsive to their own context. That would affirm their humanity and enable them to be more genuinely Christian because they would be practising a Christianity that rings true within.[32]

6.7 The Trinity as a uniting paradigm

Leaving aside the weaknesses identified, one could expect African Christianity to have its own peculiarities. It cannot, however, be seen as wrong for that reason because each region of the world has its own peculiarities in Christian beliefs and practices. It is, nonetheless, noteworthy that in trying to highlight the distinctiveness of African Christianity, I have emphasized areas of difference. In reality, the African churches and African Christians encountered here have common doctrinal positions in many areas with each other and with other churches across the world. For a start, these Africans all believe that God is Father, Son and Holy Spirit.

However, to the extent that differences exist, the diversity of theologies raises the question of how unity is to be maintained within Christianity. To pursue unity from the level of doctrine has, historically, been difficult. This difficulty has increased in recent decades because the notion of "orthodoxy" has increasingly been seen, negatively, as an imposition by coercive authority.[33] It is often the views of less powerful social groups that get labelled "heresy". For example, the Donatists, a North African movement of the late fourth and fifth centuries, who were labelled as heretics drew their membership mainly from the indigenous Berber population, whereas their Catholic opponents were mainly Roman settlers,[34] who were generally of a higher social class. Walter Bauer, who has written on orthodoxy and heresy in the early Christian churches, has noted how the concept of orthodoxy grew with the power of Rome[35] and pointed out that before the dominance of Rome, unity between the churches was not maintained at the level of doctrine but at the level of relationship with the same Lord.[36] This was in spite of the churches having their own understanding of who Christ was. [37]

Unity at the level of relationship resonates with how God in the Trinity models unity in diversity. Alongside the traditional view that the unity of God lies in the sameness of the divine substance in the three persons, a "social" understanding of the doctrine has developed in which the focus is on relationship and the persons of the Trinity are understood to have their unity not in a metaphysical substance but in their *perichoretic* relationship (i.e., their mutual indwelling). Moltmann writes:

> In respect of the Trinity's inner life, the Persons themselves form their unity, by virtue of their relation to one another and in the eternal perichoresis of their love.[38]

Those who profess and worship the Lord Jesus Christ can learn from this model, in which unity is found in fellowship (Greek, *koinonia*), and the search for Christian unity happens less in dogmatic substance and more in fellowship with one another through fellowship with Christ. From such fellowship should come a relationship of love, respect and complementarity.

6.8　Conclusion

African Christianity and its British expression raise a number of Biblical and theological issues. The evaluation of the African position on these issues shows some strengths and weaknesses. For example, its understanding of salvation has the merit of taking human physical needs seriously, but it can lead to an over-realised eschatology. An attempt was made at different stages to compare African Christianity with the forms of Christianity found in other regions to avoid evaluating the African position in a vacuum. In some cases, the same levels of weakness were discerned among African Christians and Christians from other regions. For that reason, a key theological issue was that of equality. This was argued from the point of view of the doctrine of the Trinity. Because the "persons" of the Godhead are equal to one another, and human beings are made in the image of God, human beings should see themselves as equal to one another. A second problem remained, however, which was how there could be unity in diversity. On that, the social dimension of the Trinity was seen as a paradigm. Just as in that understanding, unity is found not in substance but in the mutual indwelling of the three persons, Christians can have a Spirit-guided dialogue of mutually respecting equals from which parties can derive mutual benefits.

CHATPER 6 ENDNOTES

[1] Middleton and Walsh: 167.
[2] Ibid.
[3] Manheim: 88.
[4] Ibid: 44.
[5] Casaldinga and Vigil: 17.
[6] Ibid: 5.
[7] Takenaka: 6.
[8] Wessels: 148.
[9] Ibid.
[10] Ibid: 149, quoting Lee 86.
[11] Wessels: 156–157.
[12] Fiddes, 1989: 5.
[13] Ibid: 9.
[14] Ibid: 9.
[15] Ibid: 10.
[16] See, for example, Fiddes, 2000, 20–21.
[17] Bridger: 352.
[18] Ibid: 353.
[19] Ibid.
[20] McGrath: 195.
[21] Pattison and Woodward..: xiii.
[22] Hiltner, quoted in Pattison and Woodward: 5.
[23] Gutierrez, *Third World…*:24.
[24] Ibid.
[25] Yamauchi: 272.
[26] Gutierrez, 1996: 92.

[27] Ibid.
[28] Ibid.
[29] Gill, 1977: 32.
[30] Pattison and Woodward: 8.
[31] See, for example, Ferguson: 6.
[32] African Christian theology has largely emerged from a search for identity in Christ. See, for example, Bediako, 1992: 237.
[33] McGrath: 151.
[34] Ibid: 152.
[35] Bauer: 111–129.
[36] Ibid: 202. See also McGrath: 152.
[37] Bauer: 202.
[38] Moltmann, 1981: 177ff.

Chapter 7

Summary

My goal in this book has been to set out the nature of the Christian faith of Africans in both Africa and Britain and to contrast them to ascertain how the faith of the second group, African Christians living in Britain, was being affected by the phenomenon of living as a minority community (the Diaspora phenomenon). I looked at four areas: the use of the Bible and the doctrines of God, Jesus Christ and salvation. The investigation drew on existing studies of African Christianity in Africa coupled with my own synthesis of doctrinal positions from books recently published by African preachers, mainly from the Independent churches. In Britain, where there was little existing published study of doctrine, I had to synthesise doctrinal understanding more or less from scratch. Further information was gathered by interviewing twenty African Christians living in Britain, chosen to reflect the diversity of denominations and nationalities of Africans currently living in Britain.

I identified two sets of changes that relate to two key factors affecting African Christianity. The first is the pre-Christian worldview of Africans, which they carry into their Christian faith. This has been described as "integrated" and "holistic" because it sees the spiritual and material world as woven together and treats human beings as a whole rather than splitting them into separate aspects. This characteristic is not necessarily unique to Africa, but it is, nonetheless, a major factor in the distinctiveness of African Christianity. However, as Africans live in Britain, the British way of looking at the world and at life begins to influence them, and this in turn influences their Christian faith. The second set of changes relates to the social context. Religion does not exist in a vacuum but in a particular social context. The evidence shows that African Christians over time respond theologically to pressures coming from the British social context. One such pressure is the resistance by whites to their attempts to integrate, which they experience as racism. These two kinds of changes were identified in each of the areas examined and are set out below.

African Christians show a strong commitment to practising a Biblical Christianity. Studies show that the Bible is the centre of the life and development of African Independent Churches and that churches such as the Aladura of West Africa use all the parts of the Bible, although there is an inclination towards the Old Testament. African theologians have individually and collectively affirmed the Bible as the "basic source" of African Christian theology,[1] and African preachers faced with congregations for whom the main authority of Christian truth is the Bible tend to make frequent reference to it. Another important feature in the way Africans use the Bible is the tendency to interweave the

African Christianity in Britain

Biblical story with theirs. For example, "God changed Jacob's name to bring him good fortune…Today, God will change whatever name that is working against you."[2] Because they do not see the Bible as primarily a historical book, they have no difficulty making their story part of Biblical stories and, conversely, telling Biblical stories as if they occurred today. Part of the attraction, in the words of African theologian John Mbiti is that the Bible gives Africans "liberation from ready-made and imported Christianity, liberation to generate the kind of Christianity which more fully embraces the totality of their existence."[3]

African Christians in Britain retain, to a large extent, this attachment to the Bible. Two important differences could be linked to the change of context. Firstly, African Christians in Britain are more likely than their counterparts in Africa to use reason in addition to the Bible to support a proposition. Interviews conducted as part of the present study of African Christians in Britain showed that those who left Africa within the past five years tended to speak of the Bible in stronger terms than those who have lived in Britain for more than twenty years. For example, three people in the former group described the Bible as life or "my life." The latter were more aware of the limitation of the Bible in dealing with today's moral issues. The second change is that many Africans in Britain use the Bible to fight racism. Patrick Kalilombe has quoted Eph 4:4–5 ("one Lord, one faith, one baptism") to argue that all Christians are one[4] and Joh 11:52 (Jesus died "for the scattered children of God, to bring them together and make them one") to argue that the diversity of people in Britain foreshadows God's kingdom.[5] Pastor Matthew Ashimolowo drew extensively on the Bible in his month-long preaching against racism published in the series *Black and Blessed*.[6] In fact, more than two hundred years ago, the ex-slave, Olaudah Equiano, was challenging British Christians with the Golden Rule (Matt 7:12), "O, ye nominal Christians, must not an African ask you, learned you this from your God, who says unto you, do unto all men as you would men should do onto you?"[7]

African Christians tend to see God as a powerful being who is interested in the whole person and who will overcome the evil forces they see around them.[8] Many people have left the mission churches in Africa for AICs because the mission churches suggest that God is interested only in their souls and not in their general and total welfare, bodily and spiritual.[9] Some attributes also feature prominently in the African Christian concept of God. 1) God is commonly seen as the Creator, 2) as a Provider for people's needs in this material life, 3) as a Great Healer, which is why many churches, like the Arathi of Kenya stress supernatural healing practices,[10] and 4) as a Judge. Their attraction to the idea that God cares for both the physical and spiritual wellbeing of people, although it is Biblical, is probably also strengthened by their supernatural view of life. There is, certainly, much similarity between the post-missionary Christian concept of God and the concept of God in African traditional religion.

Much of this understanding is retained among Africans living in Britain, especially those in the AICs. Two changes, however, were discerned. A comparison of responses from Africans who have lived in Britain for

African Christianity in Britain

different lengths of time showed that those who have lived here for only a short period (five years or less) were more likely to think that all life events are a result of God's plan, whereas those who have lived here for twenty years or more tend to be more practical, regarding accidents as "part of what happens in the world". This suggested that British society makes Africans increasingly rationalistic in their understanding of life events and moves them away from the traditional African belief that physical events are usually a manifestation of spiritual realities. An even clearer sign of the Diaspora effect on the doctrine of God can be seen in the greater emphasis put on God's concern for social justice. Particularly in the historical churches, such as the Church of England, the Roman Catholic Church and the Methodist Church, the experience of racism is making African Christians relate God to ideas of human equality and diversity.

In general, Africans Christians refer to "Jesus Christ" significantly less than they refer to "God", probably because Africans have always had the concept of God in their traditional thought, whereas Jesus Christ is a new concept. The concept of Jesus shown in many studies is as a conquering warrior giving victory over various powers, such as spirits, witchcraft, magic and the devil. The sense is, "Jesus Christ is the conqueror… When we are with him we also conquer".[11] He is seen as a Great Healer giving victory over diseases and the Great Provider giving victory over material poverty. For example, the Ghanaian preacher Agyin-Asare writes that in their crusades, they "do not shout for the sick to be healed" but "make a simple demand in the name of Jesus Christ our resurrected Lord" and healing happens.[12] The

Nigerian preacher Enoch Adeboye has stated that "Jesus offers mansions and not one-bedroom flats", [13] and the Nigerian preacher, Apostle Mike Ofoegbu in *Pray Down Money*[14] recommends this prayer: "Lord Jesus, for my sake You became poor, that through Your poverty I will be rich…I will surely prosper for You have carried away my poverty and nailed it on the cross for ever."[15].

African Christians in Britain, just like their counterparts in Africa, see Jesus as their Victor (or Champion), Healer and Provider. However, a survey in 2003 by Chigor Chike showed that after living in Britain for twenty years Africans tend to think of Jesus Christ less as a Victor and more as a Forgiver of sins[16], suggesting a change of focus from external evil, with which Africans are traditionally concerned, to personal sin. Secondly, particularly in the historical churches, there is the concept that through the Cross, Jesus Christ is defeating not only personal sin but also institutional injustice, such as racism.

For example, John Sentamu, in a contribution to a Church of England booklet on racism, described how the cross of Jesus Christ brings newness of life, "not confined to personal living but radically addresses public and institutional ways of doing things. It is concerned not only with joy but also with injustice and inequality."[17] This way of using Jesus's name is, however, not yet widespread among African Christians in Britain.

Salvation has a very wide scope among African Christians. It includes within it 1) deliverance from the power of evil principalities and human enemies;[18] 2) wholeness and peace, such that one can be said to be in salvation if one is at peace with oneself, neighbours, friends and God;[19] and 3) progress in life, such as good health, a flourishing business, and having children.[20] Many Africans see these things as flowing from the Lordship of Christ and the benefit of his sacrifice:

> The Lordship of Christ is the ability of God to deliver you and make you successful. Jesus took our illness, sickness, infirmity, diseases…He took our place. He overcame them all. And because he won, we win.[21]

Unlike in the West, where the central issue of Christianity is often guilt and forgiveness, the issue for African Christians is the many dangers they see in their world.[22] So the threats are not so much within as without. Concern about sin is, primarily, not for the avoidance of guilt or the pursuit of heaven, but instead because it could hinder harmony with God and deny them God's protection and provision. As was found by H W Turner in his study of the Aladura, the cosmic conception of evil demands "a total view of salvation".[23]

British-based African Christians understand salvation, to a large extent, in the same way: as victory over human and spiritual detractors and as good health, prosperity and general wellbeing. Alongside this, however, is the understanding of salvation in socio-political terms. This can be seen in the writing of Bernard Nwulu, who lamented racism in the British National Health Service and advocated a commitment to social justice and taking risks "to alter oppressive structures"[24] and Emmanuel Lartey, who implies in his writing that black people in Britain are looking to God for the freedom to be black and protection from the "heinous sin"[25] that seeks to force them to be other than they are. The interviews of

Africans living in Britain showed that the longer African Christians live in Britain, the more they develop this social justice dimension in their understanding. One person, who has lived in Britain more than twenty years, spoke about looking to God "to uphold us in the land of the stranger" and "to get to and get through the glass ceiling that has been created due to barriers of culture, barriers of skin colour, barriers of sex". Another spoke about being "acknowledged for what we are and what we are able to do to get the reward that we deserve."

An evaluation of the findings showed that African Christianity with its particular expression in Britain has many strengths and weaknesses. Among its strengths is that it is "incarnational." In being rooted in and responsive to its context, both in Africa and Britain, it is following the model set by God in the Incarnation. For that reason, it is a Christianity that Africans can own, rather than one ready-made elsewhere. Secondly, the philosophical foundation is "an integrated view of life", which accords with much of the Bible, especially the Old Testament. One of its main weaknesses is that some of its practitioners sometimes appear to equate Christian salvation with material prosperity, an approach sometimes termed the "Prosperity Gospel". Ignoring the spiritual/eternal dimension of salvation does not reflect the breadth of the New Testament understanding and can undermine the power that the Christian hope for God's coming kingdom has on the present. Secondly, a "theology of the cross", that is knowing God as revealed through Jesus's suffering and humiliation on the cross, is lacking. Such a theology would, at the very least, provide a healthy tension to their emphasis on God's glory (*Theologia Gloriae*) and help them to cope better with unanswered prayers.

African Christianity, however, is not unique in having theological weaknesses. Insights from epistemology and sociology show that people know the world, inevitably, through their own representation and perspective and that theological position, anywhere, can be influenced by cultural, political and ecclesiastical factors. The issue then becomes that of equality, that is, whether Africans are entitled to do what Christians from other regions are doing. According to the Bible, human beings are made in the image of God (Gen 1:26–27) and this suggests that human persons be considered equal to one another, just as the persons of the Trinity are co-equal.[26] This might leave the church with the question of how to achieve unity in diversity. Here again, the social doctrine of the Trinity provides the model for moving forward. "In this social model, Father, Son and Spirit are co-equal in status and exist in a relationship of dialogue, reciprocity, self-giving and mutual love."[27] Their unity lies not in metaphysical substance but in "the eternal perichoresis of their love".[28] Christians from different parts of the world can follow God's example and find their unity in dialogue rather than seeking for it in dogma.

CHAPTER 7 ENDNOTES

[1] *African theology en route:* 192.
[2] See Ibid: 18.
[3] Mbiti, 1986: 32.
[4] Ibid: 60.
[5] Ibid: 61.
[6] Ashimolowo, *Black and Blessed*, 2004.
[7] Equiano: 27–28.
[8] Ibid.
[9] Enang, quoted in Mbiti, 1986: 154.
[10] Githieya: 240.
[11] Wessels: 94.
[12] Agyin-Asare, 2001, *Power in Prayer*: 19.
[13] Adeboye, 2002, *Jesus Lord of the Universe*: 31.
[14] Ofoegbu, 2003.
[15] Ibid: 3–4.
[16] Chike: 26.
[17] *Seeds of Hope*: ix.
[18] Ibid.
[19] Ibid.
[20] Ibid.
[21] Kayanja: 21.
[22] Mbiti, 1986: 156.
[23] Ibid.
[24] Nwulu: 235.

[25] Ibid: 83.
[26] Bridger: 353.
[27] Ibid.
[28] Moltmann, 1981: 177ff.

CHAPTER 8

CONCLUDING OBSERVATIONS

The findings of this study have implications for theology, for the Church and for Africans, especially those living in Britain. It has often been argued that Christianity and its doctrines should endeavour to reflect its context. This study shows that there is a natural process by which that happens. The way African Christians in Britain understand Christian doctrines changes over time to reflect their new context. The same phenomenon would, probably, be repeated among people of a different ethnic group. From this study, I estimate that it takes about twenty years for the influence of Western worldview to become significant. This has wider implications. Since this change in their Christian thinking is the result of the change in their philosophical context, that might be the amount of time it would, normally, take for secular ideas to find their way into Christianity. That length of time, however, cannot be an absolute figure but would depend on factors, such as the level of interaction with other cultures.

This study has implications for the Christian church, especially those churches with a worldwide communion. Since different parts of the world have substantial differences in the way they view the world, a situation where the understanding of Christian doctrines is influenced by the way a people view the world means that it would be difficult for denominations like the Anglican and the Roman Catholic Churches to maintain doctrinal uniformity. In addition to starting from a position of difference, those regions of the world could, also, be moving in different directions and would further increase the tension between the churches within that denomination. For churches like the Anglican, facing these issues, the central question becomes how unity is to be maintained.

There are also implications for Africans living in Britain. The choice they make when the come to live in Britain of what church to join becomes a choice about what kind of Christian they want to be or what kind of beliefs they want to hold. I am, myself, an Anglican. I have, however, been clear not to recommend this or any other church. Both the historical churches and the AICs have their pros and cons. The AICs help their African members to retain the African aspects of their faith, but they might in some ways be making these members less socially and politically aware and less able to face the realities of life in Britain. The historical churches have the advantage of enabling their African members to interact widely with people of other backgrounds, but their African members often encounter in the church a continuation of the racism they experience in wider society. This is perhaps why these African members of historical churches are such experts and vocal critics of racism in Britain. What is unnecessary is any kind of antagonism between these two groups. In the final analysis, both groups of African Christians are trying to hold on to the help God as they face the challenges of life in Britain.

BIBLIOGRAPHY

Adeboye, E *God the Holy Spirit* (Lagos: Christ the Redeemer's Ministries, 1997).

Adeboye, E *The Holy Spirit in the Life of Elijah* (Lagos: Christ the Redeemer's Ministries, 1997).

Adeboye, E *The Holy Spirit in the Life of Peter* (Lagos: Christ the Redeemer's Ministries, 1999).

Adeboye, E *The Water and the Fire* (Apapa: F and J Publishing, 1999).

Adeboye, E *Jesus, Lord of the Universe* (Lagos: Alpha Press, 2002).

Adeboye, E *Divine Encounter* (Lagos: Church Media Services, 2003).

Adeboye, E *Showers of Blessings* (Carrollton: One Hour Books, 2003).

Adelakun, T *Risk for Returns* (Ibadan: Victory Publishing House, 2005).

Adesogan, E *Christian Discipleship* (Jos, Nigeria: NIFES Publications, 1998).

Adogame, A "Partnership of African Christian Communities in Europe" presented at *Open Space: The African Christian Diaspora in Europe and the Quest for Human Communities*, 1999; *International Review of Mission*, Vol LXXXIX No 354, 2000, p291–298.

Aggrey-Solomon, D and Aggrey-Solomon S *The Courtship that Leads to Marriage* (Accra: Blessed Publications, 2003).

Agyin-Asare, C *Power in Prayer — Taking Your Blessings by Force* (publishers not stated, 2001).

Agyin-Asare, C *The Impact of Prayer — How to Win the Invisible War* (His Printing Hoornaar, 2001).

Akanle, G *Satan-Proof Your Children* (London: Emmanuel House, 1999).

Akanni, G *Becoming Like Jesus — God's Key to Abundant Living* (Gboko, Nigeria: Peace House Publications, 2001).

Akanni, G *The Resurrection and the Life Is Here* (Gboko, Nigeria: Peace House Publications, 2002).

Akosa, C *Fresh Anointing* (Enugu: El' Demak, 2003).

Akoto-Bamfo, K *Breaking the Power of Despair* (London: Alivia Media, 2002).

Amoo-Guttfried, K *Beginnings — The Philosopher's Stone* (London: Solid Rock, 2003).

Anderson, A "A 'Failure in Love' Western Missions and the Emergence of African Initiated Churches in the Twentieth Century" *Missiology* 29.3, July 2001.

Anyahamiwe, E *The Flesh of God* (Publisher's location not stated: Voice of the Church, 2003).

Appiah-Kubi, K "Christology" in *African Christian Theology* ed. J Parratt (London: SPCK, 1987).

Ashimolowo, M *Breaking Barriers* (London: Mattyson Media, 2000).

Ashimolowo, M *No More Excuses for Failure* (London: Mattyson Media, 2001).

Ashimolowo, M *Prevailing Prayer Against Spirits of Wickedness* (London: Mattyson Media, 2002).

Ashimolowo, M *31 Pillars of Divine Favour* (London: Mattyson Media, 2003).

Ashimolowo, M *So You Call Yourself a Man* (London: Mattyson Media, 2003).

Aulen, G *Christus Victor* (London: SPCK, 1970).

Bangkok Addembly, Official Report, (World Council of Churches, 1973).

Barker, K *New International Version Study Notes* (Grand Rapids: Zondervan Publishing House) on Pradis software.

Barrett, D *Schism and Renewal in Africa*, (Nairobi: Oxford University Press, 1968).

Bauckham, R J "Cross, Theology of" in *New Dictionary of Theology* (Leicester: InterVarsity Press, 1988).

Bauer, W *Orthodoxy and Heresy in Earliest Christianity* (Mifflintown: Sigler Press, 1996).

Bediako, K *Theology and Identity* (Oxford: Regnum Books, 1992).

Bediako, K *Jesus in Africa* (Carlisle, Cumbria: Editions Cle and Regnum Africa, 2000).

Beyond Duty (London: The Methodist Church, 2003).

Bridger "Equality" in *New Dictionary of Christian Ethics and Pastoral Care* Eds. D Atkinson and D Field (Illinois: InterVarsity Press, 1995).

Casaldinga P and Vigil, J *The Spirituality of Liberation*, (Tunbridge Well, Kent: Burns and Oates, 1994).

Castro, E *Freedom in Mission: The Perspective of the Kingdom of God* (Geneva: WCC Publication, 1985).

Racial Justice Charter (London: Catholic Association for Racial Justice, 2003).

Chike, C *Christology: The Influence of African Traditional Thinking on the Christologies of African Christians Living in the United Kingdom* (unpublished BA Dissertation, Gloucester: University of Gloucestershire, 2003).

Cone, J *The Spirituals and the Blues* (New York: Orbis Books, 1972).

Cone, J *A Black Theology of Liberation* (New York: Orbis Books, 1986).

Congress of Black Catholics (London: Catholic Association for Racial Justice, 1990).

Cugoano, O *Thoughts and Sentiments on the Evil of Slavery* first published in 1787, republished with introduction (London: Dawson of Pall Mall, 1969).

Daneel "African Independent Church Pneumatology and the Salvation of All Creation" in *International Review of Mission* 82.326 April 2006.

Dickson, K "Continuity and Discontinuity Between the Old Testament and African Life and Thought in *African Theology en Route* ed. Kofi Appiah-Kubi and Segio Torres (Maryknoll, New York: Orbis Books, 1979) p95–108.

Deya, G *Dangerous Prayers to Break Satan's Forces* (Eastbourne: Gardner's Books, 2003).

Deya, G *The Power the Wicked Cannot Prevail Against* (London: More Than Conquerors, 2003).

Deya, G *The Stronghold of Generational Curses* (Eastbourne: Gardner's Books, 2003).

Dwane, S "In Search of an African Contribution to a Contemporary Confession of Christian Faith" in *Journal of Theology for Southern Africa* 38.1, March 1982.

Ela, J *My Faith as an African* (Maryknoll, New York: Orbis Books, 1988).

Elebute, T *Open Heaven — Your Covenant Heritage* (Lagos: International Christian Faith Mission, undated).

Elisha, P M *Effective Kingdom Living — A Prophetic Perspective* (Nairobi: Kings Script Publishers, 2004).

Emmanuel, O *Maximizing Opportunities* (Lagos: Olumide Emmanuel Ministries, 2001).

Equiano, O *The Life of Olaudah Equiano* ed. Paul Edwards (New York: Longman, 1988).

Eze, C Yes, *Lord — Achieving Success Through Hearing From God* (Lagos: Consarcs, 2002).

Fashole-Luke, E "The Quest for African Christian Theologies" in *Third World Theologies* Eds. G H Anderson and T F Stransky (New York: Paulist and Eerdmans, 1976).

Ferguson, D S *Biblical Hermeneutics: An Introduction* (London: Atlanta: John Knox Press, 1986).

Fiddes, P *Participating in God* (London: Darton, Longman and Todd, 2000).

Fiddes, P *Past Event and Present Salvation* (London: Darton, Longman and Todd, 1989).

Fomum, Z T *The Way of Victorious Praying* (Mumbai: Crossroad Communication, 1988).

Frank-Briggs, E *Unbreakable Laws of Faith* (London: Emmanuel House, 2001).

Fryer, P *Staying Power* (London: Pluto Press, 1984).

Gerloff, R "African Christian Diaspora in Europe: Religious and Cultural Aspects" paper presented at the *IAMS Conference in Malaysia* 31 July–7 August, 2004.

Gerloff, R "An African Continuum in Variation: The African Christian Diaspora in Britain" in *Black Theology in Britain: A Journal of Contextual Praxis.* (Sheffield: Sheffield Academic Press, 2000).

Gerloff, R "Editorial" in *International Review of Mission*, Vol LXXXIX No 354, 2000, p275–280.

Gerloff, R "The Significance of the African Christian Diaspora in Europe" in *International Review of Mission*, Vol LXXXIX No 354, 2000, p281–290.

Gill, R *The Social Context of Theology* (Oxford: A R Mowbray, 1975).

Gill, R *Theology and Social Science* (Oxford: A R Mowbray, 1977).

Githieya, F K "The Church of the Holy Spirit — Biblical Beliefs and Practices of the Arathi of Kenya 1926–1950" in *East African Expression of Christianity* (Nairobi: East African Education Publishers, 1999) p231–243.

Greene, C *Christology and Atonement in Historical Perspective* (Cheltenham: Open Theological College, undated).

Gutierrez, G *The Theology of Liberation* (Orbis Books: New York, 1973).

Gutierrez, G *The Power of the Poor in History* (Orbis Books: New York, 1983).

Gutierrez, G in *Essential Writings* ed. Nickoloff, J (New York: Orbis Books, 1996).

Igwara, O "My Spirituality: A Spirituality of Love" in *Black Catholics Speak* (London: Catholic Association for Racial Justice, 1991) p50–58.

Jehu-Appiah, J "The African Indigenous Churches and the Quest for an Appropriate Theology for the New Millennium" in *International Review of Mission*, Vol LXXXIX No 354, 2000, 410–420.

Kabasele, F "Jesus Christ as Ancestor and Elder Brother" in *Faces of Jesus in Africa* (New York: Orbis Books, 1991).

Kalilombe, P "Race Relations in Britain — Possibilities for the Future" in *A Time to Speak* ed. Paul Grant and Raj Patel (Birmingham: CRRU, 1990) p37–45.

Kalilombe, P "My Life, Faith and Theology" in *Black Catholics Speak*, (London: Catholic Association for Racial Justice, 1991), p59–78.

Kalu, O "Church Presence in Africa" in *African Theology en Route* ed. Kofi Appiah-Kubi and Segio Torres (Maryknoll, New York: Orbis Books, 1979) p13–22.

Kayanja, R *The Patience Patient* (Kampala: Miracle Publishing, undated).

Kihiko M K *Resolving Church Splits* (Nairobi, Kings Scripts Publishers, 2004).

Kiranga, J *The Ultimate Weapon in Spiritual Warfare* (Nairobi: Men of Concerns Productions, 2004).

Kisseadoo S V A *Faith for Our Times* (Accra: Asempa Publishers Christian Council of Ghana, 2005).

Kiuna, A W *Created for Dominion* (Nairobi: Jubilee Christian Church, 2003).

Kudanjie, J K and Aboagye-Mensah, R K *Christian Social Ethics* (Accra: Asempa Publishers Christian Council of Ghana, 1992).

Kumuyi, W F *The Essentials of Christian Living* (Lagos: Zoe Publishing and Printing Limited, 1985).

Kumuyi, W F *God's 3 Fold Invitation* (Lagos: Life Press Limited, 1995).

Kumuyi, W F *ABC of Ministering Healing and Deliverance* (Lagos: Life Press Limited, 2003).

Kumuyi, W F *Joy in All Circumstances* (Lagos: Life Press Limited, 2003).

Kung, H *The Church* (Tunbridge Well, Kent: Search Press Limited, 1968).

Lema, A A "Chaga Religion and Missionary Christianity on Kilimanjaro: The Initial Phase, 1893–1916" in *East African Expressions of Christianity* ed. T Spear and I Kimambo (Oxford: James Currey Ltd, 1999).

Loewen, J "Which God Do Missionaries Preach?" in *Musicology* 14:1, Jan 1986.

Maddox, G "The Church and Cigogo: Fr Stephen Mlundi and the Church in Central Tanzania" in *East African Expressions of Christianity* ed. T Spear and I Kimambo (Oxford: James Currey Ltd, 1999).

Madugba M U *Elders at the Gate* (Port Harcourt, Nigeria: Spiritual Life Outreach Inc, 2002).

Madugba M U *Dealing with Evil* (Port Harcourt, Nigeria: Spiritual Life Outreach Inc, 2003).

Marshall, I H "Salvation" in *New Dictionary of Theology* (Leicester: InterVarsity Press, 1988).

Matynes, B *Bridges to Miracles* (Lagos: Brodaxe Publishing, 1999).

Mbiti, J *African Religions and Philosophy* (Oxford: Heinemann Educational Books, 1969).

Mbiti, J *Concepts of God in Africa* (London: SPCK, 1970).

Mbiti, J *Bible and Theology in African Christianity* (Nairobi: Oxford University Press, 1986)

Mbogori, E *Overcoming Bereavement — The Art of Dealing with Personal Loss* (Nairobi: Faith Institute of Counselling, 2002).

McGrath, A *Christian Theology an Introduction* (Oxford: Blackwell Publishers, 2001).

Mettle, H *God's Zero Theory* (Accra: Type Company Limited, 2004).

Moila, M P "God's Kingship and Value Systems in Pedi Christianity" in *Journal of Theology in South Africa* 116, July 2003.

Moltmann, J *The Trinity and the Kingdom of God* (San Francisco: Harper and Row, 1981).

Moltmann, J *The Crucified God* (London: SCM, 1974).

Mosala, J "African Traditional Beliefs and Christianity" in *Journal of Theology for South Africa* 43.1, June 1983.

Mosala, J *Biblical Hermeneutics and Black Theology in South Africa* (Grand
Rapids: Eerdmans Publishing, 1989).

Muchopa, N *Making a Difference* (London: The Methodist Church, 2001).

Muir, R D "Where Do We Go from Here: Black Christian Politics After Stephen Lawrence" in *International Review of Mission*, Vol LXXXIX No 354, 2000, p305–312.

Nathan, R "African-Caribbean Youth Identity in the United Kingdom" in *International Review of Mission*, Vol LXXXIX No 354, 2000, p349–353.

Nathan, R "African Christians United in a Unified Europe" in *International Review of Mission*, Vol LXXXIX No 354, 2000, p299–303.

Ndakwe, P *Are Africans Cursed by God?* (Nairobi: Kings Script Publishers, 2005).

Newbigin, L Proper Confidence (London: SPCK, 1995).

Ng'ang'a J *Freedom From Caged Life* (Nairobi: Neno Evangelism Centre, 2005).

Nthiga, F *A Woman of Noble Character — Who Can Find* (Nairobi: Faith Anointed Books International, undated).

Nwulu "Seeking Help with Faith or No Faith" in *Black Theology in Britain*, (The Continuum Publishing Group, 2002).

Nyamu, P K *The Holy Spirit — His Baptism* (Nairobi: Revival Springs Media, 2000).

Oborji, F A "In Dialogue with African Traditional Religion: New Horizons" in *Mission Studies* (Journal), 19.1 p13–35.

Odeyemi, E *What is the Church — A Pentecostal Perspective* (Lagos: Christ the Redeemer's Ministry, 2000).

O'Donovan, W *Biblical Christianity in African Perspective* (Carlisle: The Paternoster Press, 1996).

Odulele, A *Eternity Unveiled* (London: OVMC, 2005).

Odulele, A *God's Voice* (London: OVMC, 2003).

Odulele, A *Living by Faith — Move Your Mountains* (London: OVMC, 2003).

Oduyemi, G *Holy Living* (Lagos: Bethel Publications, 1995).

Oduyoye, M "The Value of African Religious Beliefs and Practices for Christian Theology" in *African Theology en Route* ed. Kofi Appiah-Kubi and Segio Torres (Maryknoll, New York: Orbis Books, 1979) p109–116.

Oduyoye, M *Hearing and Knowing: Theological Reflections on Christianity in Africa* (Maryknoll, New York: Orbis Books, 1986).

Ofoegbu, M *Family Liberation Prayers* (Lagos: Holy Ghost Anointed Book Ministries, 2000).

Ofoegbu, M *Pray Down Money* (Lagos: Holy Ghost Anointed Book Ministries, 2003).

Ogbonnaya, H U *The Portrait of an Ideal Christian Family* (Publishing details not stated).

Oginde, D *Possessing Your Possessions* (Nairobi: Cana Publishing, 2002).

Oha, E *Potential for Excellence* (Enugu, Nigeria: El 'Demak, 2002).

Okorocha, C "The Meaning of Salvation: An African Perspective" in W A Dyrness *Emerging Voices in Global Christian Theology* (Grand Rapids: Zondervan, 1994), p59–92.

Oludoyi, D S *Dare to Dream* (London: Emmanuel House, 2003).

Oludoyi, D S *It's Ok To Walk Away* (Shinning Light Group, 2005).

Olukoya, D K *Dealing with Unprofitable Roots* (Lagos: The Battle Cry Christian Ministries, 1999).

Olukoya, D K *Meat for Champions* (Lagos: Mountain of Fire and Miracles Ministries, 1999).

Olukoya, D K *Slaves Who Love Their Chain* (Lagos: Mountain of Fire and Miracles Ministries, 1999).

Olukoya, D K *The Lord Is a Man of War* (Lagos: The Battle Cry Christian Ministries, 2001).

Olukoya, D K *When God Is Silent* (Lagos: Mountain of Fire and Miracles Ministries, 2001).

Olukoya, D K *Satanic Diversion of the Black Race* (Lagos: Mountain of Fire and Miracles Ministries, 2002).

Onwuchekwa, E *Perilous Times and Its Consequences* (Enugu, Nigeria: publisher not stated, 2002).

Oshun C "Aladura Diaspora in Britain as a Model for Mission: A Study of Select Churches" (Unpublished paper available at the Centre for the Study of New Religious Movements, Selly Oak Colleges, Selly Oak, Birmingham).

Oshun C "Encountering Aladura Spirituality in Britain" Paper presented at the *Africa Religious Diaspora Conference*, Tetley Hall, University of Leeds, UK 7–11 Sept. 1997.

Owolabi, M *Which God?* (London: Bible Christians, 2000).

Oxford Dictionary of the Christian Church (Oxford: Oxford University Press, 1997).

Oyedepo, D *The Miracle Seed* (Lagos: Dominion Publishing House, 1985).

Oyedepo, D *Long Life Your Heritage* (Lagos: Dominion Publishing House, 1986).

Oyedepo, D *Dynamics of Holiness* (Lagos: Dominion Publishing House, 1997).

Oyedepo, D *Showers of Blessing* (Lagos: Dominion Publishing House, 1997).

Oyedepo, D *Understanding Financial Prosperity* (Lagos: Dominion Publishing House, 1997).

Ozoko, D *More Than Conquerors* (Enugu, Nigeria: Computer Edge Publishers, 2004).

Pannenberg, W *Jesus God and Man* (London: SCM, 1996).

Para-Mallam, G *Getting Into Scripture — A Fresh Approach to Re-Discovering Biblical Truth* (Jos, Nigeria: NIFES, 1996).

Parratt, J *A Reader in African Christian Theology* (London: SPCK, 1987).

Parratt, J *Reinventing Christianity* (Grand Rapids, Michigan: Eerdmans Publishing Co., 1995).

Pobee J S *Towards an African Theology* (Nashville TN: Abingdon Press, 1979).

Raboteau, A J *Slave Religion* (New York: Oxford University Press, 1978).

Resource Book: Race into the Future (Peterborough: Methodist Publishing House, not dated).

Seeds of Hope: Report of a Survey on Combating Racism in the Dioceses of the Church of England, (London: Church House, 1991).

Simotwo, J M *Towards Christian Maturity and Excellence* (Nairobi: Global Harvest and Management, 2000).

Strangers No More London (Trustees for Methodist Purposes, 2001).

Sturge, M *Look What the Lord Has Done*: (Bletchley: Scripture Union, 2005).

Takenaka, M. *God Is Rice* (Geneva: World Council of Churches, 1986).

Takon, R *Knowing and Developing Your Spiritual Gifts* (Lagos: Frontline Services, 1998).

Tetteh, T *Benefits of the Anointing* (London: L T Media Ministries, 2002).

Tetteh, L *Do Miracles Still Happen?* (London: World Miracle Outreach, 1999).

Tetteh, L *Count Your Blessings* (London: L T Media Ministries, 2002).

The Passing Winter (London: Church House Publishing, 1996).

Turner, H W *Profile Through Preaching* (London: Edinburgh House Press, 1965) p14–23.

Turner, H W *African Independent Church I and II: The Life and Faith of the Church of the Lord (Aladura)* (Oxford: Oxford University Press, 1967).

Vander-Puije, K *The Release Procedure* (Accra: Great Eagle Publications Incorporated, 2004).

Vernooij, J "Pentecostalism and Migration — The Dutch Case" Paper for the *IAMS Assembly in Malaysia,* 2004.

Wagura, P M "Karl Rahner's Theology: A Basis for Searching for an African Christianity" in *AFER* 40.1, Feb 1998.

Ward, K "Ugandan Christian Communities in Britain" in *International Review of Mission*, Vol LXXXIX No 354, 2000, p320–328.

Waritay-Tulloch, R *Emotional Rollercoaster* (London: Christ Temple, 2001).

Waritay-Tulloch, R *The Power of the Word in Your Mouth* (London: Christ Temple, 2001).

Wessels, A *Images of Jesus* (Grand Rapids, Michigan: Eerdmans Publishing Co., 1990).

Audio Sermons from African Churches in Britain

<u>Glory House, Plaistow, London (Independent)</u>

Adeferasin, Y   Title: "Walk and be Perfect" 9 Oct 05

Odulele, A   Title: "Prepare for Greatness" 21 Sept 05

Oloyede, J   Title: "Releasing Your Greatness" 2 Oct 05

<u>Kingsway International, Hackney, London (Independent)</u>

Ashimolowo, M. *Black and Blessed*, Ten Tape Series, Oct 04

"I'm Kush, I Am Not Cursed" tapes 1 & 2

"I Am Rooted, I Am Not Rootless" tape 1

"What's Gone Wrong with the Man of Colour" tapes 1, 2 & 3

"The Colour of Achievement" tapes 1 & 2

"The Coming Great Transformation" tapes 1 & 2

Ashimolowo, M   Title: "Building Your Spouse's Self-Esteem" 6 Feb 05

Ashimolowo, M	Title: "Making Progress" 8 Apr 05
Ashimolowo, M	Title: "Uncommon Blessing"
Ashimolowo, M	Title: "7 Ways To Leverage Your Life for Success" 23 Aug 04

<u>Royal Connections Church, Plaistow, London (Independent)</u>

Adeoye, C	Title: "It's Time To Shave" undated
Oludoyi, G	Title: The Divine Project" undated
Oludoyi, G	Title: What Then Shall We Say" undated
Oludoyi, S	Title: "It Is Time for Me To Succeed" undated
Oludoyi, S	Title: "Much More" undated

<u>Emmanuel Parish Church, Leyton, London (C of E)</u>

Ademola, A	Title: "Good Samaritan, Good Christians " 11 Jul 04

Ademola, A	Title: "Having the Strength To Declare Our Faith" 30 Oct 05
Ademola, A	Title: "Jesus, the One for Us" 9 May 04

<u>Victory Bible Church International, London (Independent) and its group of churches</u>

Apeagyei-Collins	Title: "What Have You Got in Your Hands" undated; Rehoboth Foundation, London (Independent)
Bamfo, O	Title: "Harvest"
Bamfo, O	Title: "The Principle of Time Management"
Cann, B	Title: "Arise and Shine" 2004 (Christ Foundation Church, London (Independent))
Cann, B	Title: "Releasing Your Potential" undated (Christ Foundation Church, London (Independent))
Sendey, V E	Title: "The benefits of forgiveness" undated

Appendix

The following people were interviewed

8 members of the African Independent Churches

4 members of the Church of England

3 members of the Roman Catholic Church

3 members of the Methodist Church

2 members of the United Reformed Church

LIST OF QUESTIONS USED DURING THE INTERVIEWS

Interviewer says:
These questions are not a test of a person's knowledge. There are no right or wrong answers. The aim is to find out what the particular person's views are as each person would have a different way of seeing things. Also, people do not have to answer any question that makes them uncomfortable.

Q1
As a Christian, what does the Bible mean to you?

Q2
Based on your experience of Christianity in Africa and here in Britain, what would you say were the main differences?

Q3
When you think of God who or what comes to mind? Who is God to you?

Q4
What about Jesus Christ? Who is Jesus to you?

Q5
From your experience of African Christians in this country, what would you say they are looking to God for?

Q6
Do you think there is a difference between how Africans worship God compared to how white people in this country worship God?

Q7
What about how people live as Christians, is there a difference between how Africans and white British people?

Q8
How would you compare African Christians in Africa with African Christians in this country?

Q9
What is your assessment; do you think there is racism in Britain?

Q10
What can the church do to tackle this problem?

Q11
Is there something you are doing in your own church?

INDEX

A

Aboagye-Mensah, R K 136
Accra 12, 128, 136, 138, 145
Adeboye, E 14
Ademola A. 147, 148
African Christianity x, xi, 1, 3, 5, 7, 9, 11–13, 24, 27, 33, 48, 54, 68, 75, 98, 105, 107, 111, 112, 118, 119, 137, 145
African Independent Churches/ AIC 3, 16, 75
African theologians 12, 33, 45, 55, 112
African tradition 33, 37
African traditional religion 37, 40, 80, 114
Aggrey-Solomon, D 17, 29, 128
Aggrey-Solomon, S 17, 29, 128
Agyin-Asare, C 128
Akanle, G 128
Akanni, G 128
Akosa 34, 129
Akoto-Bamfo, K 129
Aladura 3, 12, 26, 44, 45, 54, 74–76, 80, 112, 117, 142, 145

ancestors 3, 40, 55, 79
Anderson, A 129
Anglican 3, 28, 42, 46, 124
Anyahamiwe 17, 29, 129
Appiah-Kubi 54, 72, 77, 93, 129, 131, 135, 140
Arathi 3, 16, 26, 27, 34, 45, 72, 114, 134
Ashimolowo, M 129, 146, 147
Asian 64, 65
Atonement 69, 100, 134
Aulen, G 130

B

Bangkok Addembly 130
Barker, K 130
Barker, Kenneth 89
barrenness 79
Barrett, D 130
Bauckham, R J 130
Bauer, W 130
Bediako, K 130
Beyond Duty (Methodist Church) 74, 130
Bible x, xi, 6, 9, 11–16, 18–27, 29, 37, 40, 45, 46, 68, 80, 86, 87, 97, 111–

114, 118, 119, 137, 142, 148, 150
Black/Black People 4, 22, 23, 43–45, 51, 64–66, 74, 83–87, 88, 103, 114, 117, 120, 131, 133, 135, 138, 139, 142, 146
blackness 85
blessings 33–35, 38, 40, 77, 78, 87, 89–91, 99
breakthrough 78, 87, 88, 91
Britain/British xi, xiii, xiv, 4–7, 10, 11, 16, 17, 18, 19, 20, 21, 22, 23, 27, 30, 31, 37–42, 44, 47, 48, 53, 60–63, 65, 66, 68, 70, 71, 75, 81–83, 84–88, 91, 92, 94, 102, 107, 111–118, 123–125, 133, 135, 139, 142, 145, 146, 150, 151
business 12, 37, 57, 77, 81, 117

C

calamities 76
Casaldinga P 130
Castro 131
change xi, 15, 18, 20–22, 27, 48, 64, 66, 70, 82, 83, 86, 92, 97, 102, 113, 116, 123
Chike, Chigor ix, 116
childbearing 80
Christology/Christological 53–55, 59, 60, 63, 66–68, 72, 93, 100, 129, 131, 134

Church of England 42–44, 64, 71, 115, 116, 144, 149
colour 45, 84–86, 88, 118
Cone, J 131
Congress of Black Catholics 51, 131
cross xi, 7, 59, 61, 64, 70, 79, 100, 116, 118
Cugoano, O 131

D

Daneel 30, 55, 72, 131
death(s) 15, 54, 56, 69, 79, 81, 99
Deliverance 49
Deya, G 132
dialogue 8, 102, 103, 107, 119
Diaspora 4, 5, 7, 42, 111, 115, 128, 133, 134, 142
Dickson, K 49, 131
discrimination 5, 22, 84, 87
diversity ix, xiii, 22, 44, 84, 105–107, 111, 113, 115, 119
divorce 79
doctrine 6, 26, 42, 53, 67, 85, 101, 102, 105–107, 111, 115, 119
Dwane, S 132

E

Egypt 1, 86, 88
Elisha, P M 132
Emmanuel, O 132
enemies 68, 76, 79, 81, 89, 91, 116
Enlightenment 21, 100, 101
epistemology 98, 119

Equiano, O 132
Equiano, Olaudah 23, 114, 132
eschatology 90, 107
eternity 82
evil x, 32, 40, 54, 56, 60, 62, 65, 66, 69–71, 76, 77, 80, 81, 91, 92, 114, 116, 117
experience ix, x, xiii, 3, 5, 16, 18, 19, 21, 24, 25, 44, 46, 60, 82, 86, 88, 91, 100, 102–104, 112, 115, 125, 150
Eze, C 132

F

faith ix, xi, xiv, 5, 6, 12, 21, 25, 30, 43, 48, 53, 57, 67, 82, 89, 90, 105, 111–113, 124
Fashole-Luke, E 133
Ferguson, D S 133
Feuerbach, Ludwig 67
Fiddes, P 133
forgive/forgiveness 43, 89, 90, 117, 148
Forgiver 66, 116
Frank-Briggs 17, 29, 133
Fryer, P 133

G

Gerloff, R 133, 134
Gill, R 134
Githieya, F K 134
glory xi, 69, 70, 101, 119
Glory House 17, 29, 37, 62, 73, 146

God x, xi, xiv, 5, 6, 8, 13, 15–20, 22, 23, 26, 29, 31–49, 54, 55, 57, 59, 61–63, 67–70, 76–82, 84–92, 97, 100–107, 111, 113–119, 125, 127–129, 131–133, 136–144, 150, 151
Golden Rule 23, 114
good health 33, 34, 76, 80, 81, 91, 116, 117
Greene, C 134
Gutierrez, G 134

H

Healer x, 47, 54, 60, 66, 68, 114–116
heaven 33, 79, 117
heresy 105, 106
heritage xiv, 33, 84, 85
historical churches 43, 46, 47, 48, 65, 71, 115, 116, 124, 125
Holy Spirit 1, 14, 26, 41, 46, 105, 127, 134, 139

I

Idol worshipping 79, 86
Igwara, O 135
incarnation 118
inequality 64, 87, 116
institutional racism 84, 87
interpretation ix, x, 26, 104

J

Japanese context 99
Jehu-Appiah, J 135
Jesus Christ 8, 13, 23, 33, 40,

41, 46, 53–71, 78, 79, 83, 84, 106, 111, 115, 116, 135, 150
justice 42–44, 47, 48, 83, 87, 90, 92, 102, 115, 117, 118

K

Kabasele, F 135
Kalilombe, P 135
Kalu, O 135
Kampala 78, 135
Kayanja, R 135
KICC 65
Kihiko M 135
kingdom of God 86, 87
Kiranga, J 136
Kisseadoo 136
Kiuna, A W 136
Korean Christian 99
Kudanjie, J K 136
Kumuyi, W F 136
Kumuyi, W F Joy in All Circumstances (Lagos: Life Press Limited, 2003). 136
Kung, H 136
Kung, Hans 90

L

Lagos 127, 132, 136, 137, 139–144
liberation 16, 76, 83, 98, 103, 113
liberation theology 83, 98
life ix–xi, xiv, 2–4, 6, 12, 15–22, 24, 30, 32–37, 39, 41, 42, 44, 46, 47, 54, 58, 59, 64, 70, 76–80, 82, 86, 88, 90, 91, 92, 99, 102–104, 106, 112–116, 118, 124, 125
Loewen, J 137
longevity 80
love 14, 17, 20, 42, 44, 100, 102, 106, 119

M

Maddox, G 137
Madugba M U 137
Marshall, I H 137
materialism 88
Matynes, B 137
Mbiti, J 137
Mbogori 137
McGrath, A 138
Mental Health 83
Methodist 3, 43, 46, 51, 64, 65, 71, 115, 130, 138, 143, 144, 149
Mettle, H 138
miscarriage 79
Mission ix, 2, 128, 131, 132, 134, 135, 138, 139, 142, 145
Moila, M P 138
Moltmann, J 138
money 59, 82, 86
Mosala, J 138
Muchopa, N 138
Muchopa, Naboth 43, 64, 71
Muir, R D 138

mythology 99

N

Nairobi 9, 130, 132, 134–137, 139, 141, 144
Nathan, R 138, 139
National Health Service 83, 117
Ndakwe, P 139
Newbigin, L 139
New Testament/NT 69, 89, 91, 118
Nganga 55, 57, 72, 78, 93
Nthiga, F A 139
Nwulu 22, 30, 82–85, 94, 117, 120, 139
Nyamu 14, 28, 139

O

O'Donovan, W 140
Oborji, F A 139
Odeyemi, E 139
Odulele, A 29, 140, 146
Odulele, V 17, 29, 37, 81
Oduyemi, G 140
Oduyoye, M 140
Ofoegbu, M 140
Ogbonnaya 140
Oginde, D 141
Oha, E 141
Okorocha 77, 78, 80, 91, 93, 94, 141
Old Testament x, 14, 17, 20, 68, 86, 89, 112, 118, 131
Oloyede, J 146
Oludoyi, D S 141

Olukoya, D K 141, 142
Olukoya, D K Meat for Champions (Lagos: Mountain of Fire and Miracles Ministries, 1999). 141
Onwuchekwa 142
oppression/oppressive 23, 83, 84, 98, 117
Orthodoxy 130
Oshun C 142
Owolabi 19, 29, 142
Oyedepo, D 142, 143
Ozoko, D 143

P

Pannenberg, W 143
Para-Mallam, G 143
Parratt, J A 143
peace of mind 79
perichoretic 106
personal knowledge 26
Pobee J S 143
police 83, 84
poor 22, 23, 59, 69, 103, 116
practical theology 103
prayer 6, 34, 38, 59, 61, 62, 69, 70, 116
pre-Christian religion 40
pre-Christian worldview 70, 98, 112
preachers ix, xiii, 7, 13–15, 17, 31, 33, 36, 37, 39, 40, 57–59, 70, 75, 77–79, 82, 90, 92, 111, 112
principalities 76, 80, 116
progress 58, 76, 91, 116
prosperity xi, 35, 59, 79, 81,

82, 89–92, 117, 118
Prosperity Gospel 90, 118
Protector 41, 47
Provider x, 41, 47, 58, 60, 66, 68, 114–116
psychiatric 83
psychotherapy 83, 101
psychotic 83

R

Raboteau, A J 143
Racial Justice Charter 51, 131
racism 7, 10, 21–23, 27, 43, 44, 48, 64–66, 83, 84, 87, 102, 112–116, 125, 151
rationality 101
realism 98
reason x, 11, 15, 18, 19, 24, 27, 34, 36, 38, 40, 46, 54, 55, 100, 105, 107, 113, 118
Redeemed Christian Fellowship 33
Revival xi, 139
Roman Catholic 3, 43, 46, 115, 124, 149

S

Salvation x, 6, 75, 76, 78, 92, 116, 131, 133, 137, 141
Satan 14, 19, 57, 62, 81, 128, 132
schizophrenia 83
Seeds of Hope 43, 50, 51, 74, 120, 144

Sentamu, John 42, 44, 64, 71, 116
sickness 40, 54, 61, 69, 78, 79, 117
Simotwo, J M 144
sin 43, 48, 64, 66, 69, 77, 79, 81, 85, 89–91, 116, 117
social justice 42, 43, 44, 47, 48, 83, 87, 92, 102, 115, 117, 118
sociology of knowledge 98
song(s) 12, 33, 55, 56, 58, 63, 81
Son of God 63, 68
Soteriology/Soteriological 53, 63, 67
stereotypes 85
Sturge, M 144
suffering xi, 5, 38, 45, 62, 70, 78, 83, 89, 104, 118
survival 6, 86
sustainer 37

T

Takenaka, M 144
Takon, R 144
Tetteh, T 144
Theologia Gloriae 119
The Passing Winter 50, 144
tradition x, 4, 24, 33, 78, 103
Trinity 63, 68, 101, 102, 105–107, 119, 138
Turner, H W 145

V

Vander-Puije, K 145

Vernooij, J 145
Victor 60, 66, 69, 116, 130
victory xi, 35, 54, 56, 60–63, 69, 70, 76, 81, 115, 117
Vigil, J 130

W

Wagura, P M 145
Ward, K 145
Waritay-Tulloch, R 145
wealth xi, 34, 44, 61, 69, 80, 82, 89
wellbeing 81, 82, 89, 114, 117
Wessels, A 145
West/Western 1, 3, 5, 25, 26, 34, 54, 65, 67, 68, 75, 76, 79, 98, 100, 101, 112, 117, 123, 129
worldview 16, 27, 42, 48, 59, 70, 80, 90, 92, 97–101, 104, 112, 123
World Council of Churches 90, 130, 144
World Miracle Outreach 38, 144

Y

yin and yang 100

Printed in the United Kingdom
by Lightning Source UK Ltd.
134912UK00001B/112-156/A